"From the moment we read *Windows of the Soul* we knew Ken Gire has God's heart for the film industry. Reading *Reflections on the Movies* clearly confirms our belief.

"Ken has a rare understanding of the use and the power of the medium that few others have. He can see a film and use its messages for good, both in evaluating what the filmmaker is really saying to the viewers and in personalizing it to learn more about himself and his own life experiences through the film's characters, story, and themes.

"In *Reflections on the Movies* Ken shows by example how we should all respond to today's films—by analyzing, discussing, and vulnerably reflecting upon them, not just naively absorbing or criticizing them. We believe Ken can see films through the eyes of Jesus."

JIM COVELL, composer
KAREN COVELL, producer

Reflections *on* *the* Movies

Hearing God in the Unlikeliest of Places

❦

KEN GIRE

Victor

Cook Communications

Victor is an imprint of
Cook Communications Ministries, Colorado Springs, Colorado 80918
Cook Communications, Paris, Ontario
Kingsway Communications, Eastbourne, England

All Scripture quotations are from the *New American Standard Bible,*
© the Lockman Foundation 1960, 1962, 1963, 1968, 1971, 1972, 1973, 1975, 1977.

An effort has been made to locate sources and obtain permission, where necessary,
for the quotations used in this book. In the event of any unintentional omission,
a modification will gladly be incorporated in future printings.

Editor: Greg Clouse
Cover and Interior Design: David Carlson
Cover Photo: Tony Stone Images/Paul Conrath

1 2 3 4 5 6 7 8 9 10 Printing/Year 04 03 02 01 00

Library of Congress Cataloging-in-Publication Data

Gire, Ken.
   Reflections on the movies: hearing god in the unlikeliest of places / Ken Gire.
      p. cm. -- (Reflective living series)
   Includes bibliographical references.
   ISBN: 1-56476-673-X
   1. Motion pictures--Moral and ethical aspects. 2. Motion pictures-- Religious
aspects--Christianity. Title. II. Series.
   PN1995.5 .G55 2000
   791.43'653--dc21   00-040807

CONTENTS

"Surely the Lord is in this place, and I did not know it." —Jacob

GENESIS 28:16

DEDICATED TO

STEVE AND JULIE OLIPHINT

MIKE AND PATTI PINKSTON

DARNELL AND LESLIE BOEHM

FOR TAKING DOROTHY'S WORDS,

"THERE'S NO PLACE LIKE HOME,"

AND MAKING THEM MEAN SO MUCH MORE

THAN MERELY A MOMENT AT THE MOVIES.

INTRODUCTION

I n the preface to *The Screwtape Letters,* C.S. Lewis says: "There are two equal and opposite errors into which our race can fall about the devils. One is to disbelieve in their existence. The other is to believe, and to feel an excessive and unhealthy interest in them."[1] It seems the same could be said of the movies. One error is to live a cinematically abstinent life, in which you don't see movies at all. The other is to live a cinematically addicted life, in which all you see are movies.

These two equal and opposite errors can be seen in the film *Steel Magnolias* and in Walker Percy's novel *The Moviegoer.* "I don't see movies 'cause they're trash, and they ain't got nothin' but naked people in 'em," said the character played by Shirley MacLaine in *Steel Magnolias.* In Percy's novel the main character is at the other end of the spectrum.

> In the evenings I usually watch television or go to the movies. Weekends I often spend on the Gulf Coast. Our neighborhood theater in Gentilly has permanent lettering on the front of the marquee reading: Where Happiness Costs So Little. The fact is I am quite happy in a movie, even a bad movie. Other people, so I have read, treasure memorable moments in their lives: the time one climbed the Parthenon at sunrise, the summer night one met a lonely girl in Central Park and achieved with her a sweet and natural relationship, as they say in books. I too once met a girl in Central Park, but it is not much to remember. What I remember is the time John Wayne

killed three men with a carbine as he was falling to the dusty street in *Stagecoach*, and the time the kitten found Orson Welles in the doorway in *The Third Man*.[2]

Either extreme, I think, is a place of impoverishment. The one extreme cuts you off from a life-changing art form. The other cuts you off from life.

This most influential of art forms is a relatively modern invention that grew out of the ancient convention of storytelling. For example, notice how the Prophet Nathan confronts King David after he had committed adultery with Bathsheba.

Then the Lord sent Nathan to David. And he came to him, and said, "There were two men in one city, the one rich and the other poor. The rich man had a great many flocks and herds. But the poor man had nothing except one little ewe lamb which he bought and nourished; and it grew up together with him and his children. It would eat of his bread and drink of his cup and lie in his bosom, and was like a daughter to him. Now a traveler came to the rich man, and he was unwilling to take from his own flock or his own herd, to prepare for the wayfarer who had come to him; rather he took the poor man's ewe lamb and prepared it for the man who had come to him."

Then David's anger burned greatly against the man, and he said to Nathan, "As the Lord lives, surely the man who has done this deserves to die. And he must make restitution for the lamb fourfold, because he did this thing and had no compassion."

Nathan then said to David, "You are the man!" (2 Samuel 12:1-7)

Instead of correcting David with a lecture, Nathan came to him with a story. If you look at the story closely, it has all the drama and emotion of a feature film. Why did Nathan use this approach? He knew that a story has the stealth to slip past our defenses and find its way into our hearts. Once inside us, the story touches us. When it does, something extraordinary happens. We feel something. We may feel outrage, as David did, or any number of other emotions—fear, guilt, shame, empathy, compassion, joy, sorrow, love, hate.

A moment that touches us, whether it's a moment at church or a moment at the movies, can be a means of grace whereby God speaks to us. "I have sinned against the Lord," David said when he saw himself in the mirror of Nathan's story (v. 13). He made that confession not coming out of a temple, so to speak, but out of a theater.

A movie theater is an unlikely place to hear God. Some might say the unlikeliest of places. But if it's true, what David says in Psalm 139, that there's nowhere we can flee from God's presence; if it's true that even if we make our bed in Sheol, He is there with us; if it's true that light and dark are alike to Him; then it follows that no matter how distant the heart or how dark the theater, even there God can find us, touch us, speak to us.

PART I

The Movies

History of the Movies

Our invention can be exploited for a certain time, as scientific curiosity, but apart from that, it has no commercial value whatsoever.

LOUIS AND AUGUSTE LUMIÈRE

Two brothers in France who developed moving pictures the same time Thomas Edison did in America

My own history of the movies dates back to the mid-fifties, some forty-five years ago. This was the heyday of drive-in theaters. They were all over town. Even small towns had them. Now they are all but extinct. I know of one in Southern California. Beyond that, the only ones I have seen stand like ruins of a lost civilization, mostly in small towns that you pass through on the way to somewhere else. Looking like unkempt graveyards, most of these vacant lots still have screens, though the weather has taken its toll on them. There's a decrepit projection room with a snack bar attached. Then there are rows and rows of short poles made of scrapped drill pipe on which two speakers were mounted.

I am old enough to remember a time when most theaters showed two feature-length movies. I even remember a few serials that went along with some of them, but by that time the weekly serial had gone the way of the drive-ins.

Then there were the big "event" movies such as *Cleopatra*. One movie theater that hosted the premiere in our city remodeled the entire inside of the theater with an Egyptian motif. It was all very formal, as I remember. People dressed up. There was an intermission, like something you would expect to see at an opera. Elaborate programs were even printed, listing the actors and the characters they played.

The movies and the means of bringing them to audiences have evolved over the years. And all that's left of drive-ins and double features are memories. The history of the movies, though, spans not only the twentieth century but in a sense also the centuries before.

There is a sense in which the history of movies predates the technology that made movies possible, for ever since families sat around campfires at the end of the day, stories have been told in the dark to the rapt attention of everyone seated there. Imagine children around those campfires, looking up at their father or grandfather, standing tall and telling larger-than-life stories. Imagine the light from the fire flickering over their faces as they spoke. And imagine the stories evoking laughter, tears, even courage from all those sitting there, so still and so quiet. The closest I've come to experiencing nightly rituals such as those has been at family gatherings, where, as a child, you were mostly seen and not heard. What I heard were stories. All kinds of stories. Stories that swept me away mostly to the childhoods of my parents and relatives.

The root of all art is storytelling. Although the story may be as short as a thought or a feeling, the context of that thought or feeling constitutes a story of some kind or another. The tradition of storytelling has been passed down from generation to generation. Although the technology for telling stories has changed, our appetite for stories hasn't. The desire to be swept away by a story is so universal it almost seems encoded in our genes. In *An Experiment in Criticism,* C.S. Lewis wrote: "We want to see with other eyes, to imagine with other imaginations, to feel with other hearts, as well as with our own. . . . In love, in virtue, in the pursuit of knowledge, and in the reception of the arts, we are doing this."[1]

In his acceptance speech for the Nobel Prize, Aleksandr Solzhenitsyn said: "Archaeologists have yet to discover an early stage of human existence when we possessed no art."[2] And that includes the art of storytelling. Over the millennia, the art of storytelling has taken many forms. Adventures on land were etched in stone, baked on the outside of pottery, and painted on the inside of caves. These different art forms told stories of things like battles, buffalo hunts, and brushes with bears. Adventures at sea were etched in scrimshaw, telling tales of shipwrecks, mermaids, and sea monsters. Stories of historic wars were chiseled onto stone pillars and placed prominently around the perimeters of empires, intimidating foreigners with stories of the empire's merciless strength.

Throughout history people have always enjoyed a good story. In fact the Latin word for history is *historia,* from which we get our word "story." One of the media through which these historical stories were told was architecture. During the Middle Ages, the exteriors of buildings were divided by vertical tiers of painted windows or horizontal friezes that depicted a narrative from beginning to end. And so, what came to be known as a three-story building was one that featured three such stories on the building's exterior.

As technology increased, so did the techniques of storytelling. First came the printing press with movable type in the fifteenth century. Then, almost four hundred years later, came the picture worth a thousand words—the photograph.

In the 1820s a Frenchman named Joseph Niepce experimented with a rudimentary camera to record images on pewter. In 1839 his partner, Louis Daguerre, unveiled the images he had captured on silver-plated copper. He called them "daguerrotypes." With those images the world witnessed the birth of photography.

Thomas Edison is credited for the next technological step when he took those still pictures and made them move. He was the first person to have a film copyrighted. The year was 1894. The film, *Fred Ott's Sneeze*. And it was just that, moving pictures of a man sneezing. As insignificant as that sneeze seemed then, in time it blew the world away.

At the same time Thomas Edison developed moving pictures in America, Louis and Auguste Lumière developed them in Europe. In December of 1895, they held the first public performance of a motion picture, which premiered in Paris. Looking at their invention as nothing more than a novelty, they saw little application for this new medium.

Americans saw it differently. They went in droves to kinetoscope parlors, where they dropped a penny in the machine to view such things as a tooth extraction. With another penny they watched trained bears. With another, they watched a man sparring with a kangaroo. With still another, they watched Annie Oakley or Sandow the Strong Man.

The pennies added up to dollars. Big dollars. Seeing the popularity of moving pictures among the workaday public, filmmakers started producing longer films that eventually evolved into stories with plots that were driven by heroes and heroines fighting against insurmountable obstacles thrown at them by some villain.

The mass appeal of silent films was responsible for the birth of theaters, where large audiences could watch an entire story together instead of standing in a long line for their turn at a minute's worth of entertainment. Snippets of dialogue and "Meanwhile-back-at-the-ranch" transitions were placed on title cards that filled the screen. Music was provided by a piano or organ.

In the 1920s, all of that changed. Warner Brothers obtained financing to build a $1.5 million movie palace. With it, the studio gambled on an emerging technology—sound. In a joint venture with Western Electric, Warner Brothers presented its first Vitagraph presentation in 1926, which consisted of the film *Don Juan* and a selection of synchronized shorts that were each introduced with a drab little speech by Will Hayes. In 1927, the Warners cast Al Jolson in *The Jazz Singer,* in which he not only spoke but sang. Here is the film's review in *The New York Times* by critic Mordaunt Hall.

In a story that is very much like his own life, Al Jolson at Warners' Theatre last night made his screen debut in the picturization of Samson Raphaelson's play, "The Jazz Singer," and through the interpolation of the Vitaphone . . . the audience had the rare opportunity of hearing Mr. Jolson sing several of his own songs. . . .

Mr. Jolson's persuasive vocal efforts were received with rousing applause. In fact, not since the first presentation of Vitaphone features, more than a year ago at the same playhouse, has anything like the ovation been heard in a motion-picture theatre.[3]

Looked at as a fad at first, these "talkies" signaled the birth of a new era and the death of an old one, one that included not only silent film but vaudeville as well. In the early days of this emerging art form, stage actors looked down on the movies. So did the rich. So did the well-bred. And so did the intellectuals. Movies were looked at as entertainment for the masses, attended largely by immigrants and commoners. These people couldn't afford the stage, couldn't afford books, but even the poorest of them could find a penny here and there for moment's respite from their work-worn lives.

Part of the reason that film became the art form for the masses was because the first filmmakers themselves were immigrants and commoners. Louis B. Mayer, one of the M's in MGM, was an immigrant and a junk dealer. William Fox, of Fox Studios fame, was a cloth sponger from Hungary. Adolf Zukor, who founded Paramount, was from Hungary where he swept floors in a fur store.

The movies proved so robust as to be resistant to economic downturns, even crashes. Movies not only survived the Great Depression, they thrived during it. The still-standing Los Angeles Theater, for example, was designed in 1931 and constructed at a cost of about $1.5 million, an incredible amount at the time, some would even say an obscene amount, given the economic despair the country was experiencing. It was built to imitate the palace of Versailles, featuring massive, fluted columns, a sweeping staircase, expensive carpet, and opulent chandeliers.

Once they built it, the people came.

At a time when businesses were closing their doors in unprecedented numbers, "movie palaces" like the Los Angeles Theater were opening theirs to record attendance. Architects were asked to model these palaces after such impressive structures as the Parthenon, Louis XIV's summer home, and Far East temples. Walls were filled with original art, such as paintings by the Old Masters. Floors were filled with priceless antiques. And alcoves, with ancient sculpture. It was a decorator's dream. In 1929, one decorator named Harold Ramback remarked, "No kings or emperors have ever wandered through more luxurious surroundings."[4]

For a brief time in the 1950s the movies took a beating from a new form of entertainment—television. But by the end of the fight, the movies were still standing. With the advent of video, many thought the movies were going to take an even bigger hit. Just the opposite happened. Videos actually created a greater appetite for movies.

The movie industry has changed dramatically from its early beginnings. Instead of silent movies, we not only have sound but Surround Sound. Instead of black-and-white, we not only have color but Technicolor. Instead of movie palaces, we have multiplexes, where five, ten, sometimes twenty theaters exist under one roof.

One thing, though, hasn't changed. Our insatiable appetite for good stories. Because of that, movies are still big business. And they still have enormous influence, not only on the culture but on virtually everyone within the culture.

Influence of the Movies

All I know about life I learned from John Hughes' films.

A small bit of graffiti I found on a sign at an intersection in Hollywood (August 1999)

A similar sentiment to the quote introducing this chapter is voiced through Steve Martin's character in *Grand Canyon:* "All life's riddles are answered in the movies." An overstatement, of course. A more accurate one would be: all life's riddles are *explored* in the movies. The riddle of relationships. The riddle of romance. The riddle of adolescence, to name a few.

The riddle of adolescence is particularly explored through the films of John Hughes, who has cinematically mapped that uncertain terrain of the journey from adolescence to adulthood. Some of his films are *Sixteen Candles, The Breakfast Club, Ferris Bueller's Day Off,* and *She's Having a Baby.* The quote about Hughes' films shows the influence movies had on a single individual. But their influence extends further than that. Here are a few examples.

In 1915, D.W. Griffith's film *The Birth of a Nation,* depicting a Southern view of the Civil War, sparked race riots throughout the country.

By the 1920s, the movies had transformed America, minimizing provincial boundaries and melding the country into a cohesive whole, not only by changing personal habits but by setting societal trends. Women in the movies smoked, used makeup, cut their hair, wore stockings, and abandoned the stiff corset for the more comfortable skirt, whose hemline rose a little higher each year. As a result of these images seen coast-to-coast, entire industries flourished. Booms were seen in the cigarette, cosmetic, and rayon industries. Other industries, like corset manufacturing, floundered.

The year Clark Gable took off his shirt to reveal he wasn't wearing a T-shirt in the movie *It Happened One Night,* sales of T-shirts plummeted.

Author Salman Rushdie once said that the movie *The Wizard of Oz* made a writer out of him. Later in his life he even wrote a small book about the film.

The movie *Bambi* wreaked havoc on the deer-hunting industry. The year before the movie came out, deer hunters spent $9.5 million on licenses, tags, and hunting trips. The year after *Bambi,* sales were more than cut in half with deer hunters spending only $4.1 million.

In *Rebel Without a Cause* there were scenes of teenagers slashing tires, and Dennis Hopper, who was involved in the making of that film, said that after the film's release there were hundreds of tire slashings in neighborhoods that had never known that kind of vandalism.

John Hinckley, the man who shot President Reagan, claimed the movie *Taxi Driver* inspired him to do what he did. He felt if he shot the President, he would win the love of Jodie Foster, who starred in the movie and with whom he was obsessed.

When John Travolta danced in his white polyester suit in *Saturday Night Fever,* the whole nation went disco. Discotheques. Disco music. Disco clothes.

When Jennifer Beals wore torn sweatshirts and raggedy workout clothes in the movie *Flashdance,* women from Baltimore to Beverly Hills started wearing the same type of clothing.

When the boy in *E. T.* dropped Reese's Pieces to lure the abandoned alien, sales for the candy increased 65 percent (originally Steven Spielberg asked the maker of M&M's, but Mars refused to grant him permission).

When *Risky Business* came out, sales of the sunglasses that Tom Cruise wore in the movie skyrocketed.

The release of *Amadeus* in 1984 prompted a demand for recordings of Mozart.

A River Runs Through It single-handedly revived the fly-fishing industry.

A man working at a large Swiss bank saw some books that were slated to be shredded, looked at them, and realized they documented Jewish accounts that had been placed there for safekeeping at the outbreak of World War II. He took the books and went public with his findings. This resulted in a $1.2 billion settlement for the survivors and their beneficiaries who had had accounts at that bank. Because of the bold action he took, he received so many death threats he had to seek asylum. The reason he took such a risk? Only a few days before he had seen *Schindler's List,* and he credited the movie for giving him the courage to bring this small measure of justice to the Jewish people.

Movies have had an influence on my life as well, as I'm sure they have had on yours. Three things in my childhood are responsible for my love of movies, or picture shows, as we called them back then.

The first of those was the neighborhood where I lived the first eleven years of my life. Our neighborhood backed up to the Westerner Drive-In, and on weekends the owner let our neighborhood have the back row. We caravaned through a neighbor's backyard, loaded down with lawn chairs, blankets, a jug of lemonade, and a grocery sack full of home-popped popcorn. Looking like a Bedouin encampment, we huddled around clunky metal speakers to hear that night's movie.

On nights we didn't camp on the back row, the neighbor kids roosted on the corner curb and from there we watched that week's featured attraction. One week the show might be a western. Another week, a war picture. Another week, something scary, like *Godzilla* or *Rodan*.

We sat on that corner curb in the cool of so many summer evenings until one by one we were called home. I remember one night especially, the night when I was the last to be called. I was sitting there, watching the movie *Village of the Damned*. I'm not sure of the storyline because I couldn't hear the dialogue, but from what I could tell from the curb, the village was gradually being taken over by a group of school-age aliens who looked like normal human beings. That is, until they stared at you. When they did, their eyes glowed, and the person they stared at fell over, deader than a doornail.

I was doing fine, whistling my way through the scary parts, until a group of those children turned their eyes on the audience. One of them, no lie, looked straight at me. In an instant I knew that no amount of whistling was going to get me out of this one. When their eyes started to glow, I turned my head, jumped up, and beat feet home as fast as I could. "It's only a movie, it's only a movie, it's only a movie," I kept telling myself as I ran.

As a kid, I loved getting scared, which seems a rather sick pleasure as I think about it now. But then it was a real rush. And I loved it. I loved movies like *Invaders from Mars*, which was really scary, in spite of the fact that you could see zippers in the backs of the Martian costumes.

I loved *The Mummy* with Boris Karloff, especially those scenes where the mummy music started, signaling the fate of his next victim. As the music escalated, this dusty, loosely wrapped curse of a man trudged forward with one leg dragging behind him. All the while, you're saying to the screen, "Behind you! Look behind you! Get out of there! Hurry!" And the mummy shuffles closer, one arm reaching ahead of him to gain a choke-hold on someone's unsuspecting neck.

Or Lon Chaney in *The Werewolf,* especially when the full moon rose in the sky, and you could see the sweaty terror on his face as he was transformed from man to beast before your very eyes. Only a silver bullet could kill him, one that had to be fired, if I am remembering right, by someone who loved him. High drama. Almost Shakespearean. At least for a nine-year-old boy.

Or Bela Lugosi in *Dracula,* especially when he pulled that sweeping cape over his face and turned into a bat. Or when his eyes widened as his mouth enunciated the words, "I am Count Dra-cu-la." He could go anywhere as that bat. Maybe even in your bedroom. And the only thing that could stop him was a stake driven through his heart.

Feeling a little scared? It's starting to come back to you, isn't it? And, be honest, you're loving it!

The second influence on me during those formative years was the River Oaks Theater, an inside show. As a boy I would get dropped off there on Saturdays for the matinee. The cost for a kid? A quarter. That quarter bought you two movies, a few cartoons, and a cool respite from the summer sun. The theater was packed with kids, dropped off by parents who couldn't get a better deal on a baby-sitter anywhere, averaging out to be six or seven cents an hour. Before the movie started, kids would run up and down the aisles, chasing each other. Girls whispered among themselves about the boys. Boys giggled among themselves about the girls. As soon as the previews started, though, we scurried to our seats, where we would throw popcorn at the funnel of light coming from the projector. Then we would take our empty boxes of Pom-Poms or Junior Mints, and, with one end closed, we would put our mouth around the open end and blow, making horns out of them.

I especially remember the Saturday when a young Steve McQueen was featured there in the 1958 movie *The Blob*. I was eight. The scene I so vividly remember was the one where the blob, which was this growing glob of goo from outer space, came oozing out the small projection windows of a movie theater and onto the hysterical audience. Talk about scared. When that scene came on, everyone, and I mean everyone, in the theater screamed and turned around to see if any of that same slimy goo was coming out the projection-room windows of *their* theater.

The third influence was "All Night Movies" on channel eight. It aired Friday nights, if I remember correctly, coming on after the ten o'clock news. The placard introducing the show had a candlestick in the foreground and a television in the background. It was introduced by a man's voice, which was richly resonant, saying something like, "And now it's time for 'All Night Movies.' Our first film for tonight is (such and such), starring (so and so) and (so and so). So settle back, get comfortable, and get ready to watch . . . 'All Night Movies.'"

I can't quite remember if my parents let me stay up on those nights or if I just quietly slipped out of my room after they had gone to sleep. However I got there, by permission or subversion, I would bring a blanket and a pillow, make a snack in the kitchen, curl up on the couch, and watch until I fell asleep. The atmosphere was as much a part of the enjoyment as the movie itself. Everyone was asleep, and it was just me and the black-and-white TV, which supplied the only light. I saw all kinds of movies on those Friday nights. John Wayne, my favorite actor behind Abbott and Costello, was in many of them. *Flying Tigers. The High and the Mighty. Hondo.* And my favorite, *Shepherd of the Hills.* I liked it so much that every week I looked in the TV listings to see when it was showing next. I was in seminary before I noticed it airing again. It was scheduled for a weekday, late in the morning. I stayed home from a day of classes to watch it. I fixed myself a snack, curled up in a blanket . . . and suddenly I was a kid again.

Besides influencing me as a kid, the movies have also influenced me as an adult, especially in regard to my profession. When I wrote my first book, I was thirty, perilously late for starting a career in writing. By that time I was married with four children, and all my formal education was behind me. I knew no writers, no editors, no publishers, and precious little about writing itself. In college I had taken one course in creative writing and stopped going to class midsemester because it seemed a waste of time. Of course, by then (I was a sophomore) I had raised "wasting time" to an art form, so it was a little pretentious of me to think that way. Okay, *a lot* pretentious. Anyway, that class was my first college course on writing. It was also my last.

Ten years later, when I wrote my first book, I was convinced that this was what God wanted me to do with my life. I was determined to learn the craft however I could. My most influential mentors were movies. They were also the most fun. I studied them to see what they could teach me on a craft level. As opposed to spatial art forms like art and architecture, which we experience all at one time, movies and books are sequential art forms, ones that we experience a scene at a time, a sentence at a time. Since they are similar in form, I thought they might share some common principles.

So I observed the structure of the film, along with its plots and subplots, its themes and motifs, its rhythm and pacing, its turning points and transitions, things like that. If a movie touched me, I would read the novel from which it was adapted, attempting to get into the mind of the screenwriter to understand why certain changes had been made. Why, for instance, had a character been dropped? Why had one been added? Why was the dialogue cut short? Or new dialogue written? Why had the plot been relegated to the position of a subplot? Or the subplot elevated to the position of the plot? Why had the beginning changed, or the ending?

From this method of learning, I discovered something about myself. I was a visual learner, not a verbal one. Which translated naturally to my writing. And as I have thought about that over the years, I have come to realize that we experience life not so much through words as through images.

When we dream, we dream in images, not words. Words are symbols that point to images in the real world. The symbols themselves, however, are one step removed from the real world. And that, I think, is one of the reasons we are so drawn to movies. Unlike the written words of a book or the spoken words of a sermon, the translation has already been done for us. Because of that, nothing stands between us and the images. No snooty words we have to look up in a dictionary. No foreign phrases we have to puzzle over. No syntactically tangled sentences we need to unravel. And no paragraphs we need to go back and read again.

It's just us, face-to-face with the images, laughing together, crying together, and talking to each other about life.

Truth from the Movies

The handwritten verse that is our life is lived between the parentheses of Paradise, the one that lies behind us and the one that lies before us. Cupped in the middle, we are left longing for what we have lost and for what we will one day find.

If the root of art is storytelling, the taproots are longings. Longings for such things as truth, beauty, romance, adventure. We long to find the true north that will guide us through this life and into the next. We long to see some vestige of Paradise that hasn't been spoiled by sin. We long to love and to be loved, truly, purely, romantically. We long for something noble inside us to be wakened, rousing the hero within us to answer the call to adventure.

A screenwriter takes these abstract longings and turns them into a sequence of concrete images. Robert McKee, in his book *Story*, describes the process: "A storyteller is a life poet, an artist who transforms day-to-day living, inner life and outer life, dream and actuality into a poem whose rhyme scheme is events rather than words—a two-hour metaphor that says: Life is like this!" [1]

If life is like this, it begs a pointed and personal question: How then should I be living my life? Movies attempt to answer that question. Sometimes the answers are true. Other times they are not, telling us half-truths, even out-and-out lies.

Just as you do.

Just as I do.

And just as the Church does.

The Church is made up of so many you's and so many me's, and that is why the truth we speak there is rarely pure. It is often alloyed with cultural prejudices, denominational biases, personal opinions. And that's before we add things like jealousy, hurt feelings, pride, career advancement, greed, vengeful intentions, and peer pressure, all of which influence the truth and how we tell it.

The Church—its teachers, singers, artists, and writers—tries hard to tell the truth about life in general and about the Christian life in particular. Sometimes, though, the truth we tell is not the whole truth. We tell stories, for example, mostly from the first half of Hebrews 11, those with heroes and happy endings. Like Noah and his family being delivered from the flood. Or the Israelites passing through the Red Sea. Or men of faith conquering kingdoms and escaping the edge of the sword.

What the Church largely neglects are stories from the second half of Hebrews 11. Stories in which people of faith *didn't* escape the edge of the sword. *Didn't* get miraculously delivered. *Didn't* find their way out of the wilderness.

Given the choice, we would all want our lives scripted like the first half of Hebrews 11. But we are not given the choice. The choice is God's. Why?

Because the story is His, the stage is His, and we, who get a few brief moments on that stage, we are also His.

On that stage, most of us want to play the lead. Most of us want the best lighting, best costumes, best lines, the best of everything. We want our lives to act out a wonderful story. But our idea of a wonderful story is not the story of "a good life." It's a story of "*the* good life." With that simple revision of an article, the whole story changes. Pleased with the change, we labor under the illusion of authorship, here and there rewriting the script, typing scenes that give us health, wealth, and happiness. And, if we ever get writer's block, we can crib a few lines from the script that is written by the world, which promises those same things.

Just as the Church sometimes does.

Take these steps, and you'll be healthy. Follow this formula, and you'll be wealthy. Live this way, and you'll be happy. Those ways might be true, half-true, or an outright lie. But as a rule, truth is seldom that simple, regardless if we hear it in a church or a theater.

A truth I once heard in a theater was voiced through the film *Fatal Attraction*. Starring Michael Douglas and Glenn Close, the movie tells the truth about adultery. A profoundly biblical truth. The story illustrates the consequences of an illicit relationship, the same consequences that are told in story form in Proverbs 7.

With her many persuasions she entices him;
With her flattering lips she seduces him.
Suddenly he follows her,
As an ox goes to the slaughter,

Or as one in fetters to the discipline of a fool,
Until an arrow pierces through his liver;
As a bird hastens to the snare,
So he does not know that it will cost him his life (vv. 21-23).

Four Weddings and a Funeral, a more date-friendly movie with Hugh Grant and Andie MacDowell, tells a lie. Sitting at a table with Hugh Grant, Andie MacDowell casually runs through a list of all her sexual exploits, including those with married men. As you watch her, sitting there at the table, all smiles, the scene seduces you into believing that there are no consequences for adultery. I mean, just look at her. She's radiant. She's confident. And she's unscathed. Not an emotional scratch on her.

Leaving Las Vegas is a story about a prostitute (Elizabeth Shue) who befriends an alcoholic (Nicholas Cage) who is determined to drink himself to death. He is endearing one moment, obnoxious the next. Soft-spoken, then harsh. Good-humored, then angry. You see him in his own vomit, coughing up the lining of his stomach. Cage's portrayal puts a face on alcoholism. And it's not a pretty one. But it is a true one. Repulsively true, at times. But still true. The film shows what it's like to live not only without hope but without the hope of ever having hope. There are people all around us who are killing themselves that way. A parent. A coworker. A friend. Maybe they're not doing it as quickly or as deliberately as Cage, but they are doing it just as certainly. They will die without hope if someone who loves them doesn't intervene. Chances are, unless we know how serious a problem it is, none of us will do that. *Leaving Las Vegas* is not a movie you go to for entertainment. You go for enlightenment, to understand, if you don't know already, the abyss an alcoholic faces and how difficult it is to face that abyss alone. Understanding those things helps us to know how better to love and help our neighbor, who, without that love and help, might end up the way Nicholas Cage's character did. And it wasn't a happy ending.

Arthur, a movie starring Dudley Moore and Liza Minnelli, is also about an alcoholic. Arthur puts a different face on alcoholism. It's an endearing face, one that entertains. He slurs his words and we smile. He stumbles and we laugh. It's cute. It's funny. It's also a lie. What's so deceptive is that whenever we see a person doing some of the same things, the subliminal association we make is with Dudley Moore's character, not Nicholas Cage's. And having made it, we're more likely to be amused than to befriend.

I speak for myself and only for myself when I say this, but I would rather be told an R-rated truth than a G-rated lie. I would rather be told a story about *Ordinary People* than *Cinderella* people. Because so much more is at stake than my sensibilities and how they may be offended. Truth is at stake, which means lives are at stake. Not just physical lives but spiritual lives. And not just here and now but for all eternity.

"All Cretans are liars," quotes Paul in his letter to Titus. So are all filmmakers. And so are all Christians. Not all the time, of course. No one lies all the time. But at times we all shade the truth. And sometime or another we all even eclipse it. That is true whether we write screenplays or books, whether we produce films or sermons. So let's not be too quick to put the black hat on Hollywood and the white one on us.

Let's be fair, looking as critically at ourselves as we do at them.

Maybe then we can talk civilly to each. And, who knows, we may even enjoy it.

Criticism of the Movies

With nothing can one approach a work of art so little as with critical words;
they always come down to more or less happy misunderstandings. Things are
not all so comprehensible and expressible as one would mostly have us believe;
most events are inexpressible, taking place in a realm which no word has ever
entered, and more inexpressible than all else are works of art.[1]

RANIER MARIA RILKE

Letters to a Young Poet

Criticism is one way we can approach a movie. It seems to me, however, that this way of approaching a movie contributes little, if anything, to our growth as human beings. Critical analysis of a movie seems to me something like the way we might analyze a sentence, diagramming its subject and verb, its adjectives and adverbs, its prepositional phrases, direct objects. When we're done with the diagramming, every word is in its proper place, and there is something satisfying about that. It's the same type of satisfaction an accountant gets when he balances the books he's been examining. The difference between the two is that accounting was designed for that kind of scrutiny. Art was not. Art was designed to be experienced, not critiqued.

Criticism of works of art not only includes movies but literary works as well. And no work of literature has come under such close scrutiny as the Bible. J.B. Phillips, in the preface to his translation of the New Testament, had this to say about such an approach: "After reading a large number of commentaries I have a feeling that some scholars, at least, have lived so close to the Greek Text that they have forgotten their sense of proportion. . . . It seems to me quite beside the point to study [Paul's] writings microscopically, as it were, and deduce hidden meanings of which almost certainly he was unaware. His letters are alive, and they are moving—in both senses of that word—and their meaning can no more be appreciated by cold minute examination than can the beauty of a bird's flight be appreciated by dissection after its death." [2]

What Phillips wrote about biblical criticism can also be applied to film criticism. To analyze a film, we first have to kill it. And in killing it, we lose the sense of wonder that first caused us to crane our necks at the beauty of the film as it winged its way across the skies of our imagination.

If there is a place for criticism, it is a secondary or tertiary place, not a primary one. It should even be secondary, in my opinion, for those whose livelihood is film—writers, directors, film critics, film school instructors. We shouldn't respond to a movie critically until we have first responded to it viscerally. We should look at a movie primarily to learn something about life, and only secondarily to learn something about our livelihood.

When the Holy Spirit spoke through the writers of the New Testament, He didn't use classical Greek, the language of the educated elite. He used *koine* Greek, the language of the common people (*koine* is a Greek word meaning "common"). The common language of today is not art. It's not literature. It's film. And most people can point to a moment in a film when they have sensed God in some way speaking to them through it.

Film is the medium of the masses. Stand at a theater exit when a movie ends and notice the diversity of people leaving. Male and female. Adult, teenager, and child. Black, brown, and white. Blue-collar worker, white-collar worker, and unemployed. Wealthy, middle class, and poor. College student, junior-high student, high-school dropout. Catholic and Protestant. Christian and Jew. Atheist and agnostic. Handicapped and whole. Citizen and alien. For a couple of hours, these very different people forget their differences and come together, forming an alliance to become a nation of immigrants known as "the audience." Together they share a common experience. What brought them together and kept them together for those two hours was a movie. They came with the hope of touching the hem of that divine garment we call life, not to analyze the weave or to pick lint off the fabric.

C.S. Lewis doubted that a strictly analytical criticism of a work of art was useful, especially the type that belittled the work. Yet so much of today's criticism does just that. In his book *An Experiment in Criticism,* he shows us a different way: "We sit down before the picture in order to have something done to us, not that we might do things with it. The first demand that any work of art makes on you is surrender." [3]

As we enter the world of a movie, we subconsciously make a pact with our mind to "willingly suspend our disbelief." But C.S. Lewis suggests there is more to it than that. We must also be willing to suspend our self and everything attached to our self. Our pride. Our prejudices. Our maleness. Our femaleness. Our political leanings. Our ethnic origins. Anything that might interfere with what the work of art has to say, we are to surrender. We need to develop the patience to hear a movie out, to give it a chance to say what it has to say without interruption. Just as we would hear anyone out, without cutting him or her off midsentence.

When our Lord ate His last meal and instituted the New Covenant with His disciples, He broke bread, saying, "Take and eat; this is My body which is broken for you." We can argue whether Jesus meant those words literally or figuratively, and we can give weight to the debate with unwieldy words such as *transubstantiation* and *consubstantiation*. But we should never forget that Jesus said, "Take and eat," not "Take and critique." Jesus was offering His disciples something transcendent that came through a moment in time. And it seems to me that it was neither the time nor the place to raise a questioning hand, let alone a critical opinion. I think our experience of art, especially a movie, should be viewed something like that.

In Luke 7:36-47, there is a scene, almost like a scene in a movie, that shows how differently we see things that are right before our eyes.

Now one of the Pharisees was requesting Him to dine with him. And He entered the Pharisee's house, and reclined at table. And behold, there was a woman in the city who was a sinner; and when she learned that He was reclining at the table in the Pharisee's house, she brought an alabaster vial of perfume, and standing behind Him at His feet, weeping, she began to wet His feet with her tears, and kept wiping them with the hair of her head, and kissing His feet, and anointing them with perfume.

Now when the Pharisee who had invited Him saw this, he said to himself, "If this man were a prophet He would know who and what sort of person this woman is who is touching Him, that she is a sinner."

And Jesus answered and said to him, "Simon, I have something to say to you."

And he replied, "Say it, Teacher."

"A certain moneylender had two debtors: one owed five hundred denarii, and the other fifty. When they were unable to repay, he graciously forgave them both. Which of them therefore will love him more?"

Simon answered and said, "I suppose the one whom he forgave more."

And He said to him, "You have judged correctly."

And turning toward the woman, He said to Simon, "Do you see this woman? I entered your house; you gave Me no water for my feet, but she has wet My feet with her tears, and wiped them with her hair. You gave Me no kiss; but she, since the time I came in, has not ceased to kiss My feet. You did not anoint My head with oil, but she anointed My feet with perfume. For this reason I say to you, her sins, which are many, have been forgiven, for she loved much; but he who is forgiven little, loves little."

The woman is perceived so differently by the two men. The Pharisee sees only the surface of her life. Jesus sees beyond that to her soul. We should approach a movie like that too, not letting the off-putting things on the outside keep us from seeing the beautiful things on the inside.

When I go to the movies, I try not to critique them but to experience them, at least at first viewing. I reflect upon them, bringing them into a dialogue with God about life, and specifically about *my* life. My life with Him. My life with other people. And my life with myself. The three fundamental relationships expressed in the Great Commandment. I try to make it an honest dialogue, which is not always easy for me. To be an honest dialogue, we must be willing to admit that there are some things about which we might be mistaken. And that there are some people about whom we might have made too rash a judgment. If we're not able to say that and really mean it, we're not having a dialogue, we're having an argument, no matter how politely we voice it.

When we go to the movies, they engage us in dialogue, whether we realize it or not. Perhaps that isn't why we go, but that's what happens when we do. We go to the movies for different reasons, and often those reasons vary from occasion to occasion. But whenever we all go to the movies, we go with the anticipation of losing ourselves in someone else's story. And in losing ourselves, there is the hope that we might in some way or another find ourselves. Find something of who we are. And something of who, by the grace of God, we might become. I think it is hope, even if it is a subconscious hope, that keeps us coming back to the movies. God hopes, too, I think. I think He hopes that we might leave the theater—or the church, for that matter—a little more like the dream He is dreaming when He dreams of us.

Movies are actually closer in form to dreams than they are anything else. These celluloid dreams can be a means of entertainment, a means of enlightenment, and, in some cases, a means of epiphany.

There is, I think, a place for seeing a movie strictly as entertainment. After all, "a joyful heart is good medicine" (Proverbs 17:22). And one of the things movies does better than most media is to provide enjoyment. Some films, for example, are like cotton candy, which isn't very nutritious, but is fun to eat and satisfies a certain craving. Other films are like roller coasters, which really don't take us anywhere, but do give us one thrill of a ride. Other films are like circus clowns, which won't make a difference in our lives, but will make us laugh. And that's important. For laughter is a common grace, a gift that God has given to each and every one of us. And as Solomon said, just as there is a time to weep, there is also a time to laugh. If that is true, then there is a time for *The Way We Were* and a time for *What About Bob?* A time for *Schindler's List* and a time for *E. T.* A time for *Saving Private Ryan* and a time for *Toy Story.*

Besides entertainment, a film can provide enlightenment. It is the type of enlightenment through which we become more aware of our neighbors, more understanding of their struggles, more compassionate to their needs. Enlightenment in a movie is not simply a revelation for the sake of knowledge. In that moment of enlightenment we are called upon to change— change the way we think, the way we feel, the way we talk, the way we act, and the way we react.

Besides enlightenment, film can also be an occasion for epiphany. Just as the Holy Spirit spoke through a variety of means in the Bible, He speaks through a variety of means today. Even through movies. A scene, a character, a line of dialogue, or the movie in its entirety comes to us almost like a sacrament, and we sense the Spirit saying, "Take, eat, this is for you."

There are people who have gone into the ministry because they felt the tug of the Holy Spirit, which came to them through a scene in a movie. In my book *Windows of the Soul,* I mention a particular scene from *An Officer and a Gentleman* that helped me understand, during my stint in the wilderness, not only *what* God was doing with me but *why* He was doing it. That epiphanal moment changed the way I thought about God, the way I thought about myself, and the way I thought about my circumstances. It proved to be a turning point in my life.

Epiphany, enlightenment, even to some degree entertainment, are intensely personal. Criticism is not. Criticism is detached. We can apply criticism to a movie in a number of different ways—to find its moral center, to discover its worldview, to discuss its theme, to debate its political views, and so on. But these critiques should be secondary to the dialogue that the movie engages us in personally. A movie has something to say about life, however subtle or strange-sounding its voice.

The best way to understand what a movie has to say to us is to reflect on the moments that move us, for those moments open a window to our soul. Through that window we can look, momentarily, into the depths of who we are. What we may see is something in our past, or our future, or something in the present. We may see our hunger and our thirst. We may see our deepest fears cowering there. Or the wings of our most beautiful dreams nesting there. We may see the open sore of our woundedness. Or the beginnings of its healing. We may see our shame. Or our deliverance from that shame. We may see our sin. Or our salvation.

We may see something of heaven, calling to us. We may even see Jesus, or His shadow as He passes by. It is in those moments that we are most vulnerable to grace, when God reaches through that window, to touch us, to speak to us, to forgive us, to heal us, and to draw us closer to Himself.

Moments at the Movies

*A movie, I think, is really only four or five moments between two people; the
rest of it exists to give those moments their impact and resonance.*[1]

R O B E R T   T O W N E

Academy Award–winning screenwriter for the movie Chinatown

Movies are made up of moments. Some of those moments we remember all of our lives. Jimmy Stewart explains why:

"People will come to me and say, 'You know, there was this movie you were in, I can't remember its name, but you're in this bar, and you're very depressed, and everything's been going wrong for you, and then you look up and start saying this little prayer. I'll always remember that.'

"People remember these little moments as vividly as if they were parts of their own lives. It's all connected somehow—their lives and these movie moments.

"I know I remember movies that way, too, mostly as short moments. But these moments have had a lifelong impact on me.

"The fact that people remember these tiny moments, when they don't necessarily even remember the name of the picture or the plot, just shows that people remember the abstract idea through a human moment in the film. They don't remember it abstractly, they remember it because it had

45

some sort of emotional effect on them." [2]

Sometimes it's an entire movie that touches us, and we remember the experience as just one big moment. Other times it's a handful of moments we remember. Still other times it's maybe only one moment we carry with us when we leave the theater. How many moments touch us isn't so important as how *deeply* they touch us.

Film critic Roger Ebert describes the moment when he was first impacted by a movie. He still remembers the day in Paris—it was a rainy, summer day—when, as a college student, he saw *The Third Man,* starring Joseph Cotton and Orson Welles. Here's how describes his experience: "If there was a moment at which I understood what the movies were, and could be, it happened while I watched *The Third Man* that afternoon in Paris. I was touched on every level it is possible for a movie to touch me." [3]

In the case of writer, director, and choreographer Debbie Allen, it was one particular moment in a movie that deeply touched her: "There was no moment more relevant than Denzel Washington's performance in Ed Zwick's *Glory.* . . . The scene when Denzel is whipped for his apparent desertion (which later turned out to be nothing more than an unauthorized search for a pair of shoes that wouldn't leave his feet blistered and bloodied) captured in a few moments the pain and suffering African-Americans have endured in an ongoing struggle for human rights. The strength, dignity, and defiance of Denzel Washington's performance gave new meaning to the words *power* and *honor.* It was cinema at its best and so significant in undoing decades of wrongful images black people have been trying to overcome since *Birth of a Nation.*" [4]

Recently the American Film Institute compiled a list of the one hundred greatest movies of all time, movies that have given audiences moments they will never forget. Can you guess which movie was number one? *Lawrence of Arabia?* Guess again. *The Ten Commandments?* Not even close. *The Searchers?* No.

The greatest movie of all time, according to the American Film Institute, was *Citizen Kane.* Nominated for best picture in 1941, it didn't win, which may only prove that good movies, like good wines, get better with age. The film was directed by a young Orson Welles, who also played the leading role. The story fictionalizes the rise and fall of William Randolph Hearst, the publishing tycoon, and, in doing so, illustrates something Jesus once said, "What profit is it if a man gains the whole world and yet loses his soul?"

It was cutting-edge filmmaking at the time with its intriguing visual style, its creative transitions, its novel camera angles. One reviewer, who saw the movie when it first premiered, had this to say: "Seeing it, it's as if you never really saw a movie before: no movie has ever grabbed you, pummelled you, socked you on the button with the vitality, the accuracy, the impact, the professional aim, that this one does."

Well, all I can say is, it didn't do that to me.

Admittedly, the character study was brilliant. And certainly, the story was superbly crafted. And yes, the techniques used to tell the story were far ahead of their time. Even so, it's not my number-one movie.

To be completely unsophisticated, it's not even in my top ten.

To be shamelessly common, I don't think I would even put it in my top one hundred.

Why? Because, for me, watching the movie was strictly a cerebral experience. It never found its way into my heart. It didn't speak to me, didn't move me, didn't change me. I realize, of course, that this may say more about me than it does the movie. Even so, that was my reaction.

I had the same reaction to *Raging Bull*. The film tells the true story of the once middleweight champion of the world, Jake LaMotta, who is played by Robert DeNiro. It chronicles his rise and fall, not just as a boxer but as a human being. The film is on virtually every critic's top-ten list for the decade of the '80s. Martin Scorsese's brilliance as a director is seen in how he uses gritty dialogue, black-and-white footage, and innovative camera movements to show a man's life unraveling right before our eyes. Although differing in style, Martin Scorsese did as remarkable a job directing this film as Orson Welles did with *Citizen Kane*.

The closing scene places LaMotta in a dressing room, waiting to go on stage to entertain half-drunk people in a smoke-filled bar. He's looking at himself in the mirror, practicing his lines, which are from another story about a washed-up fighter, *On the Waterfront*. As he gets up to leave, the camera doesn't follow him. It stays on the mirror, creating a moment of reflection for the audience. Then, as the film fades to black, verses from John 9 are highlighted, a phrase at a time. Then, a phrase at a time, they fade.

So, for the second time, [the Pharisees]
summoned the man who had been blind and said:
"Speak the truth before God.
We know this fellow is a sinner."
"Whether or not he is a sinner, I do not know,"
the man replied.

"All I know is this:
once I was blind and now I can see."
John IX: 24-26, New English Bible

It was a powerful moment. It was also an epiphanal moment, a moment that sounded a hopeful note over this man's otherwise hapless life. For me, the ending was the high point of the movie. And maybe that ending justifies the means that were used to get us there. But for my money, give me a bag of popcorn, a soft drink, and a ticket to see *Rocky.* Why? Because *Rocky* moved me in ways that *Raging Bull* didn't. And the ending, though it didn't quote a Bible verse, touched me more than the Bible verse quoted at the end of *Raging Bull.*

I'm guessing now, but I don't think *Rocky* had a place on any critic's list of top ten movies for the decade. What the movie did have were moments. The most climactic of these moments was the final scene after the brutal championship bout when Rocky cried out, "Adrian! . . . ADRIAN!" Like *Raging Bull,* the ending is an epiphanal moment, too, not for the main character, though, but rather for the audience. I had bought my ticket, as I'm sure you had bought yours, thinking it was a boxing story about an underdog triumph or something along that line. The ending proved me wrong. It was a love story, because at that pinnacle moment of his career, it wasn't applause Rocky was looking for. It was Adrian.

Movies are an emotional medium, more so than any other art form. And it seems our response to them should be unapologetically emotional, which is to say, from the very depths of who we are. Behind any good movie is the heart of its creator, most likely several hearts beating as one, since film is a collaborative effort. The only worthy audience for such a work, in my opinion, is another human heart. A heart that is as eager in receiving a gift as the creator was in giving it.

Film criticism, on the other hand, is more of a cerebral response, detached from emotion. What is appealing about this kind of approach is that you can write about it, in newspaper columns, in trade journals, in books. And, you can teach it, as J. Evans Pritchart did in his introduction to a book of poetry, explaining how to graph a poem in order to determine its greatness (from a classroom scene in *The Dead Poets Society*). That's a similar kind of analysis that movies are subjected to. The story's structure can be charted on a blackboard. The character arcs can be drawn on an overhead transparency. The plot points can be graphed.

A moment that touches us in a movie is a little more elusive. It's emotional and intuitive, which makes it all the more difficult to describe. Aleksandr Solzhenitsyn explains why: "Some things draw us beyond words. Art can warm even a chilled and sunless soul to an exalted spiritual experience. Through art we occasionally receive—indistinctly, briefly—revelations the likes of which cannot be achieved by rational thought." [5]

How do we write about revelations like that? What thesaurus do we consult for experiences that lie beyond words? The best we can hope to do is not explain the moment but honor it. And the closest we can come to honoring it is with our silence. Our silence and our tears. When everything has been said about a movie that can be said, maybe it will be our silence and our tears that prove to be the truest form of criticism. And the purest.

Those moments—those wonderful untamed moments that keep us coming back to the movies—refuse domestication. We don't go looking for them as much as they go looking for us. We don't know when they will come, how they will come, or what they will do to us when they do. When they do, though, they are so achingly transcendent that criticism is too small and too stiff a wineskin to contain them.

Here and there, moments in the movies touch our most exquisite self, which is nothing less than God's masterpiece in the making. In *The Problem of Pain,* C.S. Lewis said:

We are not metaphorically but in very truth, a Divine work of art, something that God is making, and therefore something with which He will not be satisfied with until it has a certain character. Here again we come up against the "intolerable compliment." Over a sketch made idly to amuse a child, an artist may not take much trouble; he may be content to let it go even if it is not exactly as he meant it to be. But over the great picture of his life—the work which he loves, though in a different fashion, as intensely as a man loves a woman or a mother, a child—he will take endless trouble—and would, doubtless, give endless trouble to the picture if it were sentient. One can imagine a sentient picture, after being rubbed and scraped and re-commenced for the tenth time, wishing that it were only a thumb-nail sketch whose making was over in a minute. In the same way, it is natural for us to wish that God has destined for us a less glorious and less arduous destiny; but then we are wishing not for more love but for less.[6]

The intolerable complement is that we are God's workmanship

(Ephesians 2:10), and He is using all things to work together for the good (Romans 8:28) of our being fashioned into the likeness of His Son (Romans 8:29). This is what God is doing in the world. He is making you and me and all of us who love Him into living replicas of His dearly beloved Son. If that is true, it seems our only appropriate place is by His side, working as apprentices, cooperating with Him in the work He is doing in us and through us.

As Christians, we should go to the movies with the hope that after two hours in the dark we might exit the theater a little different person than when we entered it. A little more understanding. A little more compassionate. And a bit more like Jesus.

Noah benShea's book *Jacob's Journey* is a gathering of wisdom from the life of a baker named Jacob. Here is the simple but beautiful way he lived his life: "Jacob looked down at his path as if it were the current of a great river. As he stared into the flow he saw the seemingly unending line of moments given to him. Then, like a man marking a trail, he began to put his prayer between the moments, making the common profound by pausing.

"Using prayer to tie knots in time, Jacob isolated the details that would pass before others as a stream of events.

"In this way Jacob secured the moments in his life, returned their individuality, allowed the luster in each of them to be observed, and, appreciated and saved, transformed his moments into a string of pearls." 7

Jacob's way of approaching life seems a good way of approaching film as well. By taking the moments of a movie, especially the moments that move us, and putting pauses of prayerful reflection between them, the luster of each moment will be revealed. Without giving the moments those kinds of reflective pauses, we are destined—. No. The verb should be active, not passive. Without giving the moments those kinds of reflective pauses, *we destine ourselves* to superficial lives.

The following chapters are moments in the movies that made a difference in my life. I hope you enjoy them. I hope they will help you see movies as more than simply entertainment. And I hope they will bring to mind some of the moments at the movies that have made a difference in *your* life.

PART II

Reflections on Specific Movies

Reflections on *Bambi*

I know it was a cartoon, I know Thumper had one of the great scene-stealing roles, I know there was a lot of cuteness.

But I left that movie changed.

It had, and has, a terrific sense of life to it, and not life as we like it to be. You may think I'm crazy and you may be right, but Bambi *still reverberates within me.* [1]

WILLIAM GOLDMAN

Screenwriter of Butch Cassidy and the Sundance Kid, All the President's Men, *and* Marathon Man

T*itanic* has been the number-one grossing movie in history, outperforming *Star Wars, Indiana Jones,* and *Jaws.* You already know that. But do you know what the number-one movie at the box office was before all the Lucas-Spielberg blockbusters, say, before 1970?

Was it *Gone with the Wind,* with its grand sweeping scenes of the South?

Or was it *Cleopatra* with its colossal sets?

Or *The Sound of Music* with its breathtaking scenery and beautiful music?

It wasn't any of those.

It was *Bambi.*

Since its release, *Bambi* has grossed $268 million worldwide, bonding it to generations of young and old alike. But not everyone bonded to the movie. Here and there the movie has had its detractors.

For example, a reviewer, whose opinions I generally respect, had this to say about the movie: "*Bambi* is a parable about sexism, nihilism, and despair, portraying absentee fathers and passive mothers in a world of death and violence. I know the movie's a perennial classic, seen by every generation, remembered long after other movies have been forgotten. But I am not sure it's a good experience for children—especially the very young and impressionable ones."[2]

I think he arrived at those conclusions because he was a writer living on the seam of two centuries, in a world that had been influenced by the cultural issues he mentioned. The story, though, was not written at the end of the twentieth century. The author, Felix Salten, had worked on the manuscript in the 1920s, finishing it in 1928. Before the stock market crash. Before the Great Depression. Before the Second World War. The cultural context from which he was writing was one of optimism, not despair. After all, the world had finished the "war to end all wars" almost a decade earlier. When Salten wrote, the world was brimming with life and peace, not with death and violence. That was forever behind them, or so they thought then.

Another reason I think the reviewer interpreted the story as a parable of our culture is that he views the story *prescriptively* rather than *descriptively*. The story, in his opinion, prescribes a certain way of life. In my opinion, it merely describes it. The author tells a story about animals to help us see life from their perspective, with the hope that the story would sensitize us to them and to the world they live in.

"I am not sure it's a good experience for children—especially the very young and impressionable ones," said the reviewer.

I would differ with that opinion. So would Russell Banks.

Banks is an author and Princeton professor. When he first saw the movie, he was four. Very young and very impressionable. Looking back on the experience as an adult, Banks had this to say about how the movie affected him.

"I recently discovered that there was a single winter afternoon at the movies that did indeed change my life, and in such a thoroughgoing way that I am utterly unable to remember today the person I was before the moment I sat down in the Scenic Theater, the only movie house in the small mill town of Pittsfield, New Hampshire, with my younger brother Steve on one side, my cousin Neil, also younger, and Uncle Bud Eastman on the other, and the lights went out. One person—a child very much like the newborn fawn Bambi, of no particular gender, a creature whose destiny was shaped merely by his species—seems to have died that afternoon; and another—a child defined by his gender—got born." 3

Whether we grew up to be professors or priests, salespeople or stay-at-home moms, the movies in our childhood that touched us, remain with us. How could we ever forget them? How large they once loomed on the screen. How long they now linger in our subconscious. Who knows how those images have shaped us . . . or how they shape us still?

Bambi came out in 1942, before I even had a subconscious, let alone anything that could be shaped. Born in 1950, I missed the theatrical release. Years later, though, when Disney rereleased the film, I saw it. I don't remember how old I was. I do remember, though, how moved I was.

The first moment that moved me happened during the following scene.

It is a scene in which the peace of the forest turns suddenly to panic.

Startled deer are running everywhere, though from what we don't know. Until a single rifle shot cracks through the air. After Bambi and his mother are a safe distance away, the panting fawn asks, "What happened, Mother? Why did they all run?"

She pauses a moment before she answers. "Man . . . was in the forest." Which is followed by another pause that gives her words even greater resonance.

It was a sobering moment, to hear those words. I had always pictured man as a hero. Particularly the white man. Most particularly, the white, American man. When it was a story of man against a wild animal, man was the one who triumphed. And he triumphed because he was the good guy. When it was a story about the white man against the red man, the white man was always portrayed, at least in the movies, as the good guy. He was the virtuous one, the civilized one, the triumphant one. And, when it was Americans against the Germans—or against whomever we were fighting at the time—the Americans were always in the right, and, consequently, always won. Granted, that worldview is a simplistic one, but as a child, I felt safe and secure within it.

Until I heard the words: "Man . . . was in the forest."

Those words began a paradigm shift in my life, although it was so slight a shift I wasn't even aware of it at the time. Up to that point, I didn't have the ability to look through someone else's eyes, to see life from a perspective other than my own. C.S. Lewis once wrote that "Each of us by nature sees the whole world from one point of view with a perspective and a selectiveness peculiar to himself." [4] What that movie did was to help me transcend my nature, allowing me, for a brief hour and ten minutes, to hear with other ears, see with other eyes, and feel with other hearts. That, I have come to believe, is the true beginning of our growth as human beings—the ability to step out of ourselves and see the world through someone else's eyes.

It was an ability that King Arthur learned early in life from Merlin, his childhood mentor. In the movie *Camelot,* Arthur first meets Guenevere in the forest. There he tells her of his boyhood training.

Arthur: "You know Merlin brought me up, taught me everything I know. But do you know how?"

Guenevere: "How?"

Arthur: "By changing me into animals."

Guenevere: "I don't believe it."

Arthur: "There, you see? But it's true. I was a fish, a bobolink, a beaver, and even an ant. From each animal he wanted me to learn something. Before he made me a hawk, for instance, he told me that while I would be flying through the sky, if I would look down on the earth, I would discover something."

In the same way, Felix Salten lets us look at life through the eyes of a young fawn in hopes that we, too, would discover something. Through those eyes, those new and innocent eyes, we see his world as if for the very first time.

As Bambi gains confidence in his legs, he explores the alluring mystery of the world around him. What the author does for the reader is essentially what Merlin did for Arthur. He turns us into an animal. In this case, a fawn. We see the dewdropped wonder of the world through his eyes. And we process what we see through his mind.

In the book, for example, when Bambi sees a butterfly for the first time, ascending from a flower, he says, "Look, look, Mother! There's a flower flying." [5]

When he first sees a grasshopper, he says, "Look, see that piece of grass jumping. Look how high it can jump!" [6]

Then there is the moment when a group of animals talk about Man. They talk freely, even lightheartedly, until the talk shifts from Man in general to men with rifles. "But when they talked about the third hand they became serious and fear grew on them gradually. For whatever it might be, it was terrible and they did not understand it. They only knew of it from others' stories, few of them had ever seen it for themselves. He would stand still, far off, and never move. You couldn't explain what He did or how it happened, but suddenly there would be a crash like thunder, fire would shoot out and far away from Him you would drop down dying with your breast torn open. They all sat bowed while they talked about Him, as though they felt the presence of some dark, unknown power controlling them." [7]

Those words echo biblical ones chronicling the rift between man and animals that started after the Fall and deepened after the Flood.

God blessed Noah and his sons and said to them, "Be fruitful and multiply, and fill the earth.

And the fear of you and the terror of you shall be on every beast of the earth and on every bird of the sky; with everything that creeps on the ground, and all the fish of the sea . . ." (Genesis 9:1-2).

Bambi tells the story of men and animals living side-by-side in a fallen world, and serves almost as a visual aid to the verse in Genesis, explaining the uncertainty and fear that animals feel toward humans. Several of the animals in the story had seen Man in the forest, but no one could explain Him. No one could explain how he killed from such a great distance, though each had a theory.

Bambi's mother said, "He throws his hand at you, my grandmother told me."

"Is that so?" asked old Nettla. "What is it that bangs so terribly then?

"That's when he tears His hand off," Bambi's mother explained. "Then the fire flashes and the thunder cracks. He's all fire inside."

"Excuse me," said Ronno. "It's true that He's all fire inside. But that about His hand is wrong.

A hand couldn't make such wounds. You can see that for yourself. It's much more likely that it's a tooth He throws at us. A tooth would explain a great many things, you know. You really die from His bite."

"Will He never stop hunting us?" young Karus sighed.

Then Marena spoke, the young half-grown doe. "They say that sometime He'll come to live with us and be as gentle as we are. He'll play with us then and the whole forest will be happy, and we'll be friends with Him." [8]

The allusion is subtle but unmistakable. It refers to Isaiah 11:6-9, to a time of peace, not only between the animals but between the animals and man.

Between Paradise Lost and Paradise Regained is life as we now know it. That life is filled with all sorts of wonderful and terrible things, many of which are mirrored in the movies, some of which are mirrored in *Bambi.*

There are a lot of wonderful moments in *Bambi,* but there are terrible moments too. Like the moment when Bambi's mother is shot. After all these years I still remember that moment. I even remember my reaction to it.

It was the first time it had happened to me in a movie. It was the first time it had happened to me *anywhere.* I'm not sure if I cried. If I did, I didn't cry a lot or loudly. What I did do was this. I mourned. *Truly* mourned. Not just for Bambi's mother but for Bambi. Maybe even more for him.

The scene that caused me to mourn went like this. Bambi and his mother are in a meadow where the snow is just beginning to melt. Both are eating a few sprigs of grass when suddenly Bambi's mother senses danger. She lifts her head, her eyes darting over the familiar terrain, her ears listening for any unfamiliar sounds.

"Quick, the thicket," she whispers.

A shot rings out, and both are off and running.

"Keep running!" she tells him.

A louder shot sounds.

Without looking behind him, Bambi runs to the forest where snow is beginning to fall. Breathless, he looks backward, thinking his mother is just a leap and a bound behind. She isn't. He looks for her in the gathering darkness, made quiet by the drifts of snow. He calls out, "Mother . . . Mother." And each time that soft, young voice calls out, our sadness for him deepens.

The death of Bambi's mother took me by surprise. A part of me was sad.

Another part of me was shaken. After all, it was a mother that was killed. Not a criminal. Not simply an animal. A mother. What kind of world is it where mothers are killed? What kind of world is it where innocent life is indiscriminately taken? Where children are left to fend for themselves?

The *real* world.

The world we live in isn't a fairy tale. Somehow I knew that, even as a child. The world we live in isn't Cinderella's world. Or Snow White's world. Or Sleeping Beauty's. The real world is Bambi's world. What the movie had to say about life was true. Scary but true. And as strange as it sounds, knowing that was comforting. I think the movie validated the emerging feelings I had about the world I was living in. That, I think, was the source of my comfort, that I wasn't the only one who felt this way, that my truth lined up with somebody else's truth.

The film tells the truth, not only about life but about the seasons of life. It follows Bambi from birth to adolescence to adulthood, and finally, to fatherhood. We see his childhood, in all its innocence and playfulness. We see his timid curiosity as he explores the world around him. We see his sudden but shy awareness of the opposite sex when he sees the face of Faline reflected in the pond he's drinking from. We see the moment when his mother is killed. Later, we see a bullet hitting Bambi as he runs from a forest fire that nearly destroys him. We see him fighting off a pack of dogs to save Faline. We see the territorial fight for breeding rights that another young buck wages against him. Then we see Faline with a set of newborn twins, which he has fathered. Finally we see him taking his place beside his proud father, the prince of the forest. And as the father steps away, we see only Bambi, standing on an outcropping of rock and silhouetted against the sky.

The films that speak to us in our childhood have enormous resonance in our adulthood. This was underscored in my thinking when I attended The City of Angels Film Festival, where I also participated in a roundtable discussion hosted by Fuller Theological Seminary. After lunch I gave a fifteen-minute devotional for the group, showing a film clip from the movie *Smoke.*

When I was finished, one of the moderators asked if any of the audience could remember the first time when a moment in a movie touched them. One of the men, who worked for a production company, said the first movie that touched him was a French film titled *The Red Balloon.* This red, helium-filled balloon, tethered to a boy by a string, was the central character of the story. The moment that particularly touched this man was when the balloon popped and fell to the ground. As he was telling the story to this fairly sophisticated group of scholars and filmmakers, tears filled his eyes. His voice cracked at his favorite scene, the one where the other balloons huddled around the fallen one and lifted him high into the air.

That man has carried that moment with him since childhood. God only knows how it has comforted him over the years when he was feeling down, or how it has prompted him to comfort others when they have gone through some deflating experience.

I still remember movie moments that touched me as a child, moments in *The Wizard of Oz, Beau Geste, Bambi.* Every so often, one of those moments comes back to me. For instance, when we lived in Southern California, we had two rabbits living in the fenced security of our backyard. During the day they stayed mostly in the bushes. At night they came out. On moonlit nights, especially, we watched them from our bed, which headed into a screened window. One of them actually thumped the ground with his hind foot. Seeing and hearing him do that brought back Thumper and all his cuddly cuteness and his so-sweet-it-makes-you-smile dialogue.

"Watcha gonna call him?"

"Kinda wobbly, isn't he?"

Along with Thumper came Bambi. And along with him came all the warm, childhood memories I had of this film. Maybe that is why I said yes when my kids wanted those two rabbits for pets.

I didn't always view rabbits as pets. I viewed them as targets.

As a boy, I grew up loving to fish and to hunt. The hunting started with a slingshot, then a BB gun, a pellet gun, and later a .22. I shot varmints mostly. Skunks. Armadillos. Possum. I also shot a lot of birds. And rabbits.

But only one deer.

While I was hunting with a friend, I saw a good-sized buck, but I didn't have a good shot, so I saved it. We were leaving that afternoon, and I didn't want to come home empty-handed. The only deer I saw was a doe. Getting it in my crosshairs, I fired.

One bite to the shoulder, and it was dead.

Left behind, startled and turning every which way in their confusion, was a set of twins, not yet weaned. To them it wasn't an "it" I had killed. It wasn't even a "she." It was a mother, their mother.

What sense could they have made of the man with the third hand? Or of the sudden and permanent absence of their mother?

I shot a gun only once after that. And having shot it, I never one again.

Why? Who can say? Maybe it was the image of those two fawns, stumbling over themselves, stopping, sniffing the air, turning around, going a few yards then stopping, tentatively changing directions, looking so confused and so scared.

Or maybe it was the image from the movie. The image of little Bambi all alone in the forest, calling for his mother. Searching everywhere. Not finding her. Not knowing what had happened to her. Calling out to the gathering darkness, "Mother . . . Mother."

Or maybe it was the image of our two youngest children who were twins, just toddlers at the time.

Or maybe somewhere in my subconscious, all three of the images somehow merged. I don't know. All I know is that now, whenever I see a deer, I think of Bambi.

And whenever I think of Bambi, it evokes the tenderest and gentlest of feelings. Feelings I think we all will have, all the time, when, at last, the wolf will lie down with the lamb (Isaiah 11:6-9). When, at last, we will no longer hurt or destroy. When, at last, we will live with the deer and be as gentle as they are, existing together in peace, playing together as friends.

Then, at last, the whole forest will be happy.

And God will be happy too.

Reflections on *Camelot*

*The world now consumes films, novels, theatre, and television in such quanti-
ties and with such ravenous hunger that the story arts have become humanity's
prime source of inspiration, as it seeks to order chaos and gain insight into life.
Our appetite for story is a reflection of the profound human need to grasp the
patterns of living, not merely as an intellectual exercise, but within a very personal, emotional experience.* [1]

ROBERT MCKEE

Story

C *amelot* was a stage play before it was a movie. I saw the movie when
I was a freshman in college. I was married with four kids before I
saw the play. The play, oddly enough, didn't move me, at least not as the
movie did. And the movie moved me, I think, as I look back on it now,
because I saw in it what I couldn't see on stage.

Close-ups.

Through the eye of the camera I could see the sparkling of Arthur's eyes,
the trembling of Lancelot's hand, the quivering of Guenevere's lips. And the
beginnings of all of their tears. The camera captured the slightest emotion
that flickered across their faces, creating an intimate bond between the
actors and the audience.

I loved the movie when I first saw it, and that love has deepened over the past thirty years. So much so, that it is now one of my top five favorites. Part of my love for the movie has to do with the richness of the era in which the story takes place. It is a time of kings and knights, of lofty ideals and noble deeds, of castles and round tables and jousting tournaments. What kid, regardless of age, wouldn't love that?

The story itself is heartbreaking. It's the story of a king, those who loved him, and those he loved, who were the very ones that betrayed his love. The story is filled with pageantry, chivalry, and nobility. In the end, though, it is filled with tragedy. Lancelot's affair with the queen destroys the Round Table and everything it ever stood for.

As tragic as its ending, a ray of hope shines in the final scene. Immediately preceding that scene, King Arthur communicates his forgiveness to his betrayers, who were his dearest friend and his dearest love. You see something of the forgiveness when Arthur grasps Lancelot's hand, holding it firmly as he looks into his eyes. And you *hear* something of the forgiveness when he tells Guenevere good-bye. The sadness of the scene is overwhelming. Lancelot walking away in tears, off to battle where he will play out the consequences of his sin. Guenevere taking another way, also in tears, off to the convent where she will live out her own consequences.

As the queen leaves, the camera focuses on Arthur's face. He is regal in his reserve, resolved to be a king and not a man. Yet it is a man's heart that is broken. And it is a man's words that are spoken. The words, spoken softly to himself, are as tender as they are tragic.

"Good-bye, my love . . . my dearest love."

The pain you feel for him, for all of them, is too great to bear without

70

the shoulders of tears. The king stands for a moment in silence until Guenevere is gone, then is jostled out of his silence by a rustling sound behind a nearby tent.

"Who's there? Who's there? Come out, I say!"

A frightened young boy, no older than twelve, emerges from behind the tent: "Forgive me, Your Majesty. I was searching for the sergeant of arms and got lost. I didn't wish to disturb you."

"Who are you, boy? Where did you come from? You ought to be in bed. Are you a page?"

"I stowed away on one of the boats, Your Majesty. I came to fight for the Round Table. I'm very good with the bow."

"And do you think you will kill people with this bow of yours?"

"Oh yes, Milord. A great many, I hope."

"Suppose they kill you?"

"Then I shall be dead, Milord. But I don't intend to be dead. I intend to be a knight."

"A knight?"

"Yes, Milord. Of the Round Table."

"When did you decide upon this nonexistent career? Was your village protected by knights when you were a small boy? Was your mother saved by a knight? Did your father serve as a knight?"

"Oh, no, Milord. I had never seen a knight until I stowed away. I only know of them. The stories people tell."

"From the stories people tell you wish to be a knight? What do you think you know of the knights and the Round Table?"

"I know everything, Milord. Might for right! Right for right! Justice for all! A Round Table where all knights would sit. Everything!"

Arthur walks away, then suddenly he turns, his eyes lit with excitement. "Come here, my boy. Tell me your name."

"It is Tom, Milord."

"Where is your home?"

"In Warwick, Milord."

"Then listen to me, Tom of Warwick. You will not fight in the battle, do you hear?"

Suddenly disappointed, the boy replies: "Yes, Milord."

"You will run behind the lines and hide in a tent till it is over. Then you will return to your home in England. Alive. To grow up and grow old. Do you understand?"

"Yes, Milord."

"And for as long as you live you will remember what I, the king, tell you; and you will do as I command."

Tom's eyes come alive: "Yes, Milord."

Arthur speaks some of the stanzas of the song he sang to Guenevere earlier in the movie. Only the words are different now. So are the ears that hear them. The words are addressed to Tom, and after the first stanza, the words turn to song.

Each evening from December to December
Before you drift to sleep upon your cot,
Think back on all the tales that you remember
Of Camelot.

Ask ev'ry person if he's heard the story;
And tell it strong and clear if he has not:
That once there was a fleeting wisp of glory
Called Camelot. . . .

As Arthur approaches the end of the song, his voice slows and lowers:

Don't let it be forgot
That once there was a spot
For one brief shining moment that was known
As Camelot . . .

When Arthur is finished singing, he asks his old friend Pellinore to bring him his sword, which he uses to knight the boy, "Sir Tom of Warwick." Pellinore breaks in, questioning the king as to what he is doing and reminding him he has a battle to fight.

Filled with hope, Arthur replies: "Battle? I've won my battle, Pelly. Here's my victory. What we did will be remembered. You'll see, Pelly. Now, run, Sir Tom! Behind the lines!"

Tom, full of radiance, says: "Yes, Milord."

And as the boy runs, Arthur calls out to him: "Run, Sir Tom! Run, boy! Through the lines!"

"Who is that, Arthur?" asks Pellinore.

"One of what we all are, Pelly. Less than a drop in the great blue sea. But it seems some of the drops sparkle, Pelly. Some of them do sparkle!"

Camelot is made up of moments. And some of those moments sparkle. Some of them *do* sparkle. Especially that final moment.

But it was not the final moment that touched me the first time I saw the film in 1969. It wasn't until years later, when I myself had become a writer of stories, that the scene found a place to live in my heart. And it found a place to live in my heart because, in a very real sense, I was Tom, a boy sent behind the lines. A boy who had no teacher and no training. A boy who had no skill or self-confidence. All he had were stories. Stories and the commission of a King, who, for reasons the boy couldn't understand at the time, had faith in him to write them.

The stories of King Arthur and the Round Table have been passed down from generation to generation. If you go back far enough, you will find a real, historical figure. Arthur was a six-century warrior who was a defender of the Christian faith. His most noted accomplishment was bringing together all the separate kings and land barons of Britain and forging them into a confederacy dedicated to the ideals of bravery and chivalry, law and order, truth and justice, goodness and mercy.

For centuries the stories of King Arthur and his heroic deeds were preserved only through the oral tradition of professional storytellers. A collection of these stories, called *The Mabinogion,* was compiled around A.D. 1050. Then in 1135, Geoffrey of Monmouth took the stories and wove them into a single, historical account. Geoffrey's work was written in Latin and translated into numerous languages, spreading the stories throughout the entire civilized world. About the same time, French poets versed their own stories of King Arthur. And in 1176, Walter Map organized all the Arthurian legends in the form we have them today.

The stories traversed the centuries. In 1203, Wolfram von Eschenbach wrote *Parzival*, a German epic poem that contains one of the most important accounts of the Arthurian legend of the Holy Grail. Throughout medieval times, wandering minstrels kept the memory of Arthur alive by going from town to town staging theatrical renditions of the story, which audiences loved.

Toward the end of the medieval era, shortly before the printing press came to England, Sir Thomas Malory wrote *Le Morte d'Arthur*. Three years later in 1477, in Westminster, England, William Caxton printed the English translation of Malory's work, giving it even greater distribution. Malory's stories are the ones upon which Tennyson based his epic poem, *Idylls of the King*, which was published in installments from 1835 to 1885.

After that, poets such as Matthew Arnold and Algernon Swinburne used the Arthurian stories as a source for their poetry. Wagner and Debussy composed operas about them.

Next in the literary lineage, T.H. White wrote *The Once and Future King*, the story that formed the basis for the play *Camelot*, which first appeared at the Majestic Theatre in New York City, December 3, 1960. The play and lyrics were written by Alan Jay Lerner, and the music was composed by Frederick Loewe. It was adapted as a movie in 1969, starring Richard Harris and Vanessa Redgrave. The first time I heard the story of Camelot was through that movie.

Numerous books have been written about King Arthur. One of them I have in my library, titled *King Arthur for Boys*, by Henry Gilbert. It has no date of publication, but the personal inscription indicates it was a gift, given on Christmas, 1930.

In the preface of the book the author writes: "This book is an attempt to tell some of the stories of King Arthur and his Knights in a way which will be interesting to every boy and girl who loves adventures. . . . No doubt many of you, my young readers, have at some time or another taken down the *Morte D'Arthur* from your father's bookshelves and read a few pages of it here and there. But I doubt if any of you have ever gone very far in the volume. You found generally, I think, that it was written in a puzzling, old-fashioned language, that though it spoke of many interesting things, and seemed that it ought to be well worth reading, yet somehow it was tedious and dry.

"In the tales as I have retold them for you, I hope you will not find any of these faults. Besides writing them in simple language, I have chosen only those episodes which I know would appeal to you." [2]

My point in tracing the genealogy of these stories is this: Generations ago, some boy ran behind the lines and lived. He lived and he told stories. He was a *teller* of stories at first, then a *writer* of them. Through his words the stories were remembered, inspiring other boys and girls who also ran behind the lines to keep the stories alive. For fifteen hundred years, the stories lived and continue to live to this day because of them.

That is the storyteller's mission. And it is a noble mission.

Although it doesn't always seem that way.

Being a writer, at times, seems a coward's profession, some level of desertion from the foot soldiers on the front lines. Whether running behind the lines is an act of cowardice or heroism depends, I think, on several things.

Whose command sent us running.

What stories we write once we stop.

And why we write them.

At some time or another, I have been the coward, letting other people command me, telling stories that don't merit retelling, and doing it for such trivial reasons as personal gain or professional expediency.

Other times, though, I have heard the call of the King, so loudly and so clearly, that keeping the stories alive seemed not only the most heroic of missions but also the most noble of professions.

Each generation must think back on all the tales that it remembers. And tell them. The King James translation told those stories in words that people in the seventeenth century understood. Today we are puzzled by the old-fashioned language. Even sermons about those stories, sermons just a century old, now seem tedious and dry. That is why the stories must retold in a simple language its audience can understand, whether that audience consists of curious children, country farmers, or college professors.

To us—to you and me and all of us who have been knighted by the King—the commission has been given to keep alive the greatest story ever told.

You and I know of Christ from the stories people have told. The faith we have came from hearing them. The stories have been passed from one generation to another. Stories of one brief shining moment when the earth was graced with the presence of its once and future King.

Reflections on *Amadeus*

A *madeus* is one of the worst titles ever given a feature film. Or . . .

It is one of the best.

The title is taken from Mozart's middle name, and it is as oblique a word as it is obscure. Who of us, before the film came out, even knew Mozart's middle name? And of those who did, who knew its meaning?

The meaning can be found by dividing the name into syllables and tracing their Latin roots. *Ama* means "beloved." And *deus* means "God." Together they mean "Beloved of God."

If the title were chosen to spotlight the central character, it was a poor choice because the name is unrecognizable to the average moviegoer. Other movies with one-word titles, such as *Jaws* or *Titanic,* have immediate name recognition. The titles alone are catalysts to visually compelling marketing campaigns.

But if you're the one responsible for marketing this movie, what do you do with a title like *Amadeus?* What direction could you possibly give the person who is supposed to design the poster? What advertising hook could you possibly come up with to overcome a title from a language that hasn't been spoken for centuries?

Amadeus.

It's a marketing nightmare.

It's also a writer's dream.

Every writer dreams of an intriguing title that will encapsulate the story's central conflict in as few words as possible. Which is what this one does. In a word, it tells what the film is about.

It's about God and His grace and our jealousy over how He bestows it.

All of these themes meet in Mozart, God's beloved.

Salieri, a contemporary of Mozart and a composer of lesser talent, is the character who carries the jealousy theme. It is his story, not Mozart's. In the film, Salieri is the court composer to Emperor Joseph II. The conflict begins in 1781, when Mozart arrives to play for the emperor's court. When he finishes, the court is astounded. It is then Salieri realizes that the gift he has sought from God for so long has been given to another. To Mozart.

For Salieri, the giftedness of Mozart is proof that he, and not Salieri, is the one who is "beloved of God." Yet Mozart's character is filled with arrogance, temperamental fits, raucous carousings, drunkenness, sexual immorality, and irreverence. Which raises a theological question for Salieri. How could God withhold such a gift from someone as deserving as he and give it to someone as undeserving as Mozart?

Don Campbell, author of *The Mozart Effect*, writes of the gift that Mozart received:

A gifted performer from the age of four, Mozart was one of the most famous child prodigies in history. Like young Jesus, who amazed the elders in the temple, young Wolfgang astonished the royal heads of Europe; and musicians, composers, and audiences everywhere applauded his youthful brilliance and virtuosity. He first composed a minuet and trio for the keyboard when he was six years old, and his last piece came 626 major compositions later. By the time he was twelve, he was writing constantly, creating in the course of his career seventeen operas, forty-one symphonies, twenty-seven piano concertos, dozens of piano sonatas, and music for organ, clarinet, and other instruments. He could imagine one piece as he wrote down another; he seemed to see a whole composition before he committed it to paper. In a letter to his father, he explained, "Everything has been composed but not yet written down." [2]

Clearly it was an extraordinary gift. But it was a gift that Mozart neither longed for, nor asked for, nor even seemed grateful for. In the end, it is the caprice of God in how He bestows His gifts that drives Salieri not only to madness but to murder.

In the opening scene of the movie, the guilt-ridden Salieri cuts his throat with a razor and is taken to an asylum. Sometime later, a priest visits him there. This is their conversation, which frames the central conflict of the movie.

The priest enters the asylum, which is a menagerie of insanity, and picks his way through the maddening crowd of inmates to Salieri's room. He enters to the sound of the elderly composer playing a small piano.

Salieri stops and turns to the intruder. "Leave me alone."

"I cannot leave a lonely soul in pain," replies the priest.

"Do you know who I am?"

"That makes no difference. All men are equal in God's eyes."

Salieri pauses before responding. "Are they?" His question betrays his cynicism.

"Offer me your confession," says the priest. "I can offer you God's forgivenness."

Salieri changes the subject. "How well are you versed in music?"

"I know a little. I studied it in my youth."

"Where?"

"In Vienna."

"Good," says Salieri, turning to his piano. "Then you must know this." And he plays one of his compositions.

When he finishes, the priest is apologetic. "I can't say that I do. What is it?"

"It was very popular," Salieri answers, then turns to another composition. "How about this?" As he plays, the music transports him to his glory days as court composer. When he finishes, he's enraptured by the applause. Opening his eyes, he turns to the priest, expectantly. "Well?"

"I regret it is not too familiar."

"Can you recall no melody of mine? I was the most famous composer in Europe. I wrote forty operas alone. Here, how about this one?" And once again he plays.

As he does, the priest's eyes come alive with recognition, and he starts mouthing the notes. When Salieri stops, the priest responds enthusiastically.

"Yes, I know that. That's charming. I'm sorry, I didn't know you wrote that."

"I didn't. That was Mozart. Wolfgang *Amadeus* Mozart," he says, his voice putting a slightly sneered emphasis on the middle name.

"The man you are accused of killing," says the priest, his face turning suddenly grave.

"You've heard that?"

"Is it true? For God's sake, my son, if you have something to confess, do it now. Give yourself peace."

Salieri reflects, almost wistfully. "He was my idol. Mozart. I can't think of a time when I didn't know his name. When I was still playing childhood games, he was playing music for kings and emperors, even the Pope at Rome." Salieri returns in his memory to the boy he once was, all the while continuing his conversation with the priest. "I admit, I was jealous when I heard the tales they told about him. Not of the brilliant little prodigy, but of his father, who had taught him everything. My father did not care for music. . . . How I wished I could be like Mozart. How could I tell him what his music meant to me? While my father prayed earnestly to God to protect commerce, I would offer up, secretly, the proudest prayer a boy could think of."

As the old Salieri says this, the young Salieri looks at a crucifix on the wall, and bows his head to pray. "Lord, make me a great composer. Let me celebrate your glory through music . . . and be celebrated myself. Make me famous through the world, dear God. Make me immortal. After I die, let people speak my name forever with love for what I wrote. In return, I will give you my chastity, my industry, my deepest humility, all the days of my life. Amen."

It is a painful encounter for Salieri, his encounter with that priest. Here he is at the frayed end of his life, and it is Mozart's music that proves to be immortal. It is his melody the priest remembers, his music that brings light to the priest's eyes.

The entire film is Salieri's confession to this priest, chronicling an ongoing dialogue that he has had with God over the course of his life. Only it seems less of a dialogue and more of a monologue. And that can be seen as far back as his childhood prayer, which seems more a haggling over a shopkeeper's price than a dialogue with God about his life and how he should be living it.

When it is apparent to Salieri that God isn't living up to His end of the bargain, his heart hardens. So much so, that when he asks, "Why would God choose an obscene child to be His instrument?" it is less of a question and more of an accusation.

Later, the accusation becomes more explicit. "You are unjust, unkind," he says to the crucifix he's holding. "From now on, we are enemies." And he throws the crucifix into the fire. From that point on, Salieri not only pits himself against God but plots revenge against Mozart, God's beloved.

There are natural and inevitable consequences to jealousy. Eventually jealousy, in a moment of stealth, slips out of the heart to walk among the shadows where it waits for its moment of revenge. The revenge may come in a back-stabbing moment of criticism. Or in a character-assassinating moment of gossip. But whenever it comes, however it comes, it comes to kill.

Salieri's jealousy killed everything he once held dear in his life. In the end, he hated God, hated Mozart, hated even himself. You feel his self-loathing at the end of the movie when he dubs himself "the patron saint of mediocrity."

The movie touched me, but not the way *Camelot* did. Its touch was more like a poke in the eye, and I didn't like it. Nothing about it felt good or the slightest bit uplifting.

When I first heard the call of God, commissioning me to write, I responded like the newly knighted Sir Tom of Warwick. I ran behind the lines to tell stories. I ran with a mission. I wrote with a passion. And I prayed with enthusiasm. "Make me a good writer, dear Lord. Let me serve You through my writing."

And then . . .

I grew up.

Along the way to growing up, I lost my innocence about writing. It was too hard, too frustrating, too disappointing, too painful. I questioned myself, questioned my calling, and questioned the One who had called me. The questions drew me into a dialogue with God, which grew more intense the longer the questions went unanswered. After a while, the questions went from "How can I serve You, Lord?" to "Why aren't You living up to Your end of the bargain?"

Something of Salieri is in those questions. But I never knew it until I saw the movie. The movie showed me what jealousy looked like, what it sounded like, and how it would destroy you in the end if you didn't destroy it first.

Before the movie, I wouldn't have thought jealousy was an issue in my life. And in many ways it isn't. I don't struggle with jealousy over the gifts that God gives to other people. I am never jealous of a writer when I read a really good book. I never wish that I had been the one who had written it. I never wish that I had the skill of the writer who had written it. I struggle with plenty of things in my life, but not those things.

What I do struggle with is this. I work hard at what I do. And I've worked hard for a long time. Because of that, whenever I hear of some first-time author writing a novel on a whim, and the novel not only becomes a best-seller but is going to be made into a movie, I struggle to rejoice in that writer's good fortune.

The Bible says I should. And I wish I could. But it's hard.

It's hard because nothing about writing has come easy for me. Not learning to write. Not the actual writing. Not finding an agent. Not finding a publisher. Not finding an audience for my writing. Nothing has come easy. And so when a book comes along, say, for instance, a book like *The Bridges of Madison County*—first book the author ever wrote, and it's not only a best-seller but gets made into a movie—it stirs up a lot of old questions and a lot of old feelings attached to those questions.

I hate it when I hear myself asking those questions. Especially those questions about the movies.

Because of my long-term love of the movies, when I started writing, I wanted to write stories that could be made into movies. I prayed. I took classes. I studied. I wrote screenplays. I contacted agents, friends of agents, producers, acquaintances of producers, people who once thought they saw a producer in a restaurant. I tried everything. And nothing has come of it. That is why the following words are so difficult for me to hear.

"All I ever wanted was to sing to God," said Salieri. "He gave me that longing. And then made me mute. Why? Tell me that. If He didn't want me to praise Him with music, why implant the desire?"

On a good day, I tell myself that maybe the longing will be fulfilled in God's own time, and I just need to be patient. Or I tell myself that maybe I have misinterpreted the desire. Maybe my love of movies was given by God to teach me to be a better writer, or a better person. Who knows?

On a bad day, though, the Salieri who lives in me raises a question. As he speaks, I understand his pain more than I understand why God would give me the longing and make me mute.

This much I do understand. All good gifts come from the generous hand of God. And He distributes those gifts however He wants. In return He asks only that we are grateful in receiving them and faithful in exercising them.

I know these things to be true.

Even so, Salieri still lives.

Reflections on *Field of Dreams*

I think that Shoeless Joe [Field of Dreams] changed some people, how they look at the world, how they feel about themselves and their families.[1]

PHIL ALDEN ROBINSON

Interviewed in American Screenwriters *by Karl Schanzer and Thomas Lee Wright*

I t has been said that each generation must grow its own corn and write its own stories. Besides writing its own stories, each generation has also been entrusted with the stories from previous generations. When we dress these hand-me-down stories in new clothes, they are able to walk among a new generation of readers, and the stories seem as fresh as the day they were written.

The Parable of the Prodigal Son is one of those stories. In *Heidi*—both the book and the movie—the reading of the biblical parable is a turning point in the story at which the reclusive grandfather returns to God and to the village he once left. The delightful children's book, *Where the Wild Things Are* by Maurice Sendak, is another example. In act one, the ungrateful boy is at home, sentenced to his room without dinner. In act two, he travels in a dream to a place where there are no parents, a place "where the wild things are." In act three, the boy wakes from the dream and is home again, this time with a change of heart. The story has the same theme and structure as the Prodigal Son. In act one, the ungrateful prodigal is at home. In act two, he is in a distant country, living it up. And in act three, he returns home, humble and repentant. The movie *Field of Dreams* is yet another retelling of the Prodigal Son, only it's the father who leaves and returns to the son rather than the other way around.

The backdrop of *Field of Dreams* is baseball, but the story isn't so much about baseball as it is about a reunion between a son and his father. The son's name is Ray Kinsella, a baby boomer looking back on his life. The father's name is John, a one-time minor league ballplayer whose sole link to his son was baseball.

The film begins with a series of photographs and 8mm films that chronicle Ray's journey from childhood to parenthood. Ray narrates over the pictures, and as he does, we learn of his gradual estrangement from his father. By age ten, Ray hated baseball. By age fourteen, he refused to play catch with his father and shelved his glove forever. By age seventeen, he got in a fight with his father and left home. He never saw his father again. Dad died before either of them could mend the fences in their relationship.

The incident that starts the story happens as Ray is walking through the cornrows of the Iowan farm that he and his wife, Annie, have purchased. It is there he hears a mysterious voice: "If you build it, he will come." He stops and looks around, but no one is there. Again the voice speaks. "If you build it, he will come." Ray doesn't know where the voice is coming from, what it wants him to build, or who will come once it's finished. The voice comes a third time. "If you build it, he will come."

With those seven words, Ray sets off on a life-changing journey, though this reluctant traveler doesn't have a clue where it will take him. When Ray sees a fleeting vision of a baseball diamond, he suddenly understands what the voice meant.

After Ray finishes the ball diamond, White Sox legend Shoeless Joe Jackson walks through the outfield wall of cornstalks and onto the field. Soon other ballplayers from Shoeless Joe's team join him.

To externalize the pain of Ray's loss, the author uses the image of eight White Sox players who had been banned from ever playing in the big leagues again as a consequence for plotting to throw the 1919 World Series.

Shoeless Joe, the team's spokesman, describes the pain: "Getting thrown out of baseball was like having a part of me amputated. I've heard that old men wake up scratching their legs that have been duffed for fifty years. I'd wake up at night, smell of the ballpark in my nose, feel of the grass on my feet. . . . Man, I loved this game. I'd have played for food money. It was the sounds, the smells. Ever held a glove to your face? I'd have played for nuthin'."

Soon Ray receives another revelation. With the voice's cryptic words, "Ease his pain," Ray is off again, trying to figure out who has the pain and why it needs easing. He goes to the library, where he scrolls through spools of microfilm until he finds the person he's looking for—Terrance Mann (J.D. Salinger in the book). Ray tracks down Mann, but when Ray explains why he is there, Mann thinks he is crazy and tries running him off. But Ray is persistent. He takes Mann to a baseball game where he sees something flash across the electronic scoreboard. It is the name and statistics of a ball-player nicknamed "Moonlight Graham." Along with them is a new fragment of revelation: "Go the distance."

Seeing the same vision, Mann joins Ray, and the two are off on another leg of their journey, the quest to find Moonlight Graham. The three finally end up back in Iowa, where Shoeless Joe and the others are playing ball. At the end of the game, Shoeless Joe comes up to Ray, points to the catcher, and says: "If you build it, *he* will come." A flash of recognition crosses Ray's face. It's his dad. And he's young again, lean and wiry, with his whole future ahead of him.

The building of the field wasn't only for Shoeless Joe's return. It was for Ray's dad. And the words, "Ease his pain," which first referred to Terrance Mann's pain, now is given new meaning by Shoeless Joe. "It was you, Ray." It was *Ray's* pain that needed easing, the pain caused by the sudden loss of his father, closing the door on any possibility of restoring the relationship. The double meaning of the words is something like a messianic psalm such as Psalm 22. On one level the words of the psalm refer to David, while on another level they refer to the Messiah.

Ray's father comes to thank him for the field, asking if this is heaven. To which Ray replies, "It's Iowa." The meeting is awkward, and Ray is at a loss for words. His father turns to go. But before he leaves, Ray calls out: "Hey, Dad," and his voice cracks. "Wanna have a catch?"

The father turns to face him. "I'd like that."

And as they toss the ball back and forth, the healing begins. And when the camera pulls back and pans upward, we see a caravan of cars, their headlights on, weaving their way to this field of dreams. At the moment the camera panned upward, I was blindsided with emotion. I ached for my own dad to return. And I ached, I think, for something else, for the place where dreams come true. Heaven. And I ached for something of that heaven to touch the few acres of land that is my life the way it had touched Ray's.

I was so moved by the movie, especially the ending, that I bought the book upon which it was based. I got the name of the book from the movie's credits—*Shoeless Joe* by W.A. Kinsella. And through it I was able to experience the themes of the movie on an even deeper level.

In *Field of Dreams* Ray's dad doesn't come till the end of the movie, but in the book he returns about two-thirds of the way through the story. Phil Alden Robinson, the director of *Field of Dreams,* who also wrote the screen adaptation from Kinsella's novel, suggested saving the entrance of Ray's father until the last scene to make the story more of a mystery and so the ending would be a surprise not only to Ray but to the audience. It's one of the few times that a change in a novel's ending by Hollywood actually made the story more poignant.

The movie came out three years after my father passed away, and that is why the ending was so emotional for me. I suspect it was for anyone who has ever loved and lost a father and longed to have him back again, if only for a game of catch. The movie made me realize not only how important that father-son relationship is, but also how tenuous. It can be severed in a second by a stroke, car wreck, heart attack. Then all that remains, for better or for worse, are memories.

Because of the way the movie affected me, I thought about it a lot. And the more I thought about it, the more I began to see some biblical parallels. At that point my dialogue with the film shifted from me to my faith, especially in regard to a life of faith and hearing the voice of God.

The novelist E.L. Doctorow once said that writing a novel is like driving at night with your headlights on; you can see only a few feet in front of you, but you can make the entire trip that way.

Living a life is like that too. Especially a life of faith.

Before we ever set out on a trip like that, most of us want to see not only where we are going but what we are going to encounter along the way. We want to know where the scenic overlooks are, the dangerous turns, the drop-offs, what stretches of road are under construction and what detours we will have to take to avoid them, what towns we'll pass through, what places of interest. We want to see the entire trip at a glance, how far we have to travel and how much it's going to cost to get us there.

In short, we want a road map.

What we are given, instead, is a spiritual version of a AAA TripTik, which reveals only the next stretch of road immediately ahead. God gave Abraham a similar TripTik when He spoke to him with instructions that were as cryptic as those given to Ray: "Go forth from your country, and from your relatives and from your father's house, to the land which I will show you" (Genesis 12:1). Turning to the New Testament, we hear an echo of that call: "By faith Abraham, when he was called, obeyed by going out to a place which he was to receive for an inheritance; and he went out, not knowing where he was going" (Hebrews 11:8).

"Go to the land which I will show you."

And Abraham went out, not knowing where he was going.

Ray Kinsella's response to the voice that found him that day in a cornfield illustrates God's call to Abraham. God revealed to Abraham only the part of the map he needed to see at the time. The revelation was piecemeal but progressive (Genesis 12:1; 13:14-17; 17:1-21). Just like the revelation that was given to Ray ("If you build it, he will come." . . . "Ease his pain." . . . "Go the distance.") Ray didn't get the second bit of revelation until he stepped out in faith by acting on the first. The same pattern held true for Abraham. And the same holds true for us. Seldom, if ever, are any of us given a glimpse of our spiritual journey in its entirety. It comes in fragments, like pieces of a puzzle. And it is left to us to turn the pieces over in our minds and fit them together.

That same pattern of piecemeal but progressive revelation can be seen in the way the Messiah was revealed. The revelation starts out obscurely but grows clearer with each piece. The first piece of the puzzle came in Genesis 3:15, when God told Eve that, though her seed would be bruised by Satan, in the end it would triumph over him. Another piece came in Genesis 12:1-3, when God told Abraham that through his seed all the nations of the earth would be blessed. In 2 Samuel 7:12-16, another piece is turned over and fit into the puzzle, revealing that this Messiah would come through David's line and would establish an everlasting kingdom. Isaiah 7:14 states that this coming king would be born of a virgin. Isaiah 61:1 tells us that the Messiah's ministry will largely be with the afflicted and the brokenhearted. The piece in Micah 5:2 gets specific, identifying the village of Bethlehem as the place where He would be born. Matthew 1:21 gets even more specific, revealing the Promised One's name to be Jesus.

The revelations given to Ray are remarkably diverse. Through an articulate voice only he can hear ("If you build it, he will come."). Through visions (the baseball diamond and later, the scoreboard). Through a dream (which his wife also had). Through a fellow traveler (Terrance Mann). And through an otherworldly messenger (Shoeless Joe).

When I first began to think about how these diverse revelations came together, the method seemed, pardon the pun, out in left field. That is, until once again I put the story in dialogue with the Bible. When I did, the movie seemed almost a visual aid to Acts 9–10, which is a sequence of scenes regarding Paul and Peter and their respective ministries to the Gentiles and the Jews.

In Acts 9:1-9, a mysterious voice calls out to a group of travelers on the road to Damascus. "Saul, Saul, why are you persecuting Me?" The voice identifies itself as Jesus. Saul has been blinded by a bright light, and his companions lead him to Damascus. In Damascus a man named Ananias is given a vision (vv. 10-18). In the vision the Lord instructs him to find Saul and lay hands on him so his sight can be restored. The words mystify Ananias because of Saul's reputation for persecuting Christians was so notorious. But the Lord assures him that there is no mistake, that Saul is a chosen instrument of His to witness to the Gentiles.

In faith, Ananias goes on what he must think is the strangest mission ever. Once he finds Saul, Ananias says: "Brother Saul, the Lord Jesus, who appeared to you on the road by which you were coming, has sent me so that you may regain your sight, and be filled with the Holy Spirit" (v. 17). After that, Saul goes to Jerusalem to associate with the disciples, but, as you can imagine, the disciples are leery. The story seems too bizarre to be believed (v. 26).

In Acts 10:1-8, the focus shifts from Paul to Peter. In those verses, the believing Gentile, Cornelius, is given a vision. In the vision an angel of God tells him to go to Joppa and find Peter. What the angel doesn't tell Cornelius is why. Meanwhile in Joppa, Peter is on a rooftop, praying, and it is there he sees a vision, telling him he can now eat unclean animals (vv. 9-16). As Peter reflects on the vision, the Holy Spirit speaks to him, informing him that three men are looking for him (vv. 17-20). When Peter goes downstairs, he sees Cornelius and two other men (vv. 21-22). When Cornelius tells Peter about his vision (v. 30), Peter suddenly realizes that God has declared Gentile believers to be on equal footing with Jewish believers, rendering them clean, just like the animals in his vision. God validates their acceptance into the body of Christ by having the Holy Spirit poured out on the Gentiles who are there with Peter (vv. 31-48).

The reason why God reveals His will in such a piecemeal manner is that it helps us realize that we can't possibly have His will entirely figured out as we can figure out a road map. Because God parcels out these bits of revelation to other people, we need to come together with those people in order to put the pieces of the map together. The piecemeal revelation serves to make us not only more dependent on God but on each other. When we do come together, sharing what God has given us, a community of faith is formed. In that community each member is important, and each member desperately needs the others. What we are seeing come together in Acts 10 is the earliest formation of the body of Christ.

None of the pieces makes a lot of sense until the end, when they have all been put together. In the end, in a moment of epiphany, everything becomes clear. And there is no clearer illustration of this process than in the movie *Field of Dreams*.

As I reflected on this passage of Scripture and on the movie, suddenly I realized why God sometimes works in such mysterious ways. Because He not only wants to get us to a certain place, He wants to develop in us, en route, the characteristics of humility and faith. He wants us to become not only more dependent on Him, but also more dependent on each other. That is how a community of faith is formed—out of the humbling realization that we not only desperately need God, but we desperately need each other.

Reflections on *Ordinary People*

I saw this movie in my early thirties. What an incredible effect it had on me. Everything I grew up with was happening before my eyes. They made a movie of my life. Other people said the same thing. Then I realized that's why it's called Ordinary People, *because to some lesser or greater degree this movie is about all of us.*[1]

GARY SOLOMON

The Motion Picture Prescription

Films take us places we have never been before, transporting us around the world and across the centuries. They have taken us somewhere in time, back to the future, and around the world in eighty days. They have taken us out of Africa, on a trip to Bountiful, and to Austrian hills that were alive with the sound of music. They have taken us to the jungles of Vietnam, the beaches of Normandy, and the 'hoods of south central Los Angeles. They have taken us over the rainbow, under the volcano, and into the perfect storm. They have taken us on a voyage to the bottom of the sea, a journey to the center of the earth, and to a galaxy far, far away.

Of all the places the movies have taken us over the years, there is one place that by and large they have passed over.

Home.

Not Dorothy's home in Kansas, where she longs to return. Or Kevin's home in the suburbs, where he is left alone. But an ordinary home. In an ordinary neighborhood. With ordinary people.

Wonderfully directed by Robert Redford, *Ordinary People* is the story of a family in crisis. There are no guns. No car chases. No special effects. The actors are not screen idols or teen idols. There is no witty, sitcom dialogue. And there is no Hollywood ending.

Everything about the movie is ordinary.

Which is what makes it so extraordinary.

The film is an adaptation of a book by Judith Guest. It tells the story of a family in crisis, bobbing in the emotional wake of a tragic boating accident. The two brothers in the family had been sailing together when a sudden storm capsized their boat. Buck, the more athletic brother, drowns. Conrad (Timothy Hutton), the younger brother, survives. And having survived, he is left to cope not only with the tragedy but with the guilt of being alive. He doesn't cope well. After attempting suicide, he is treated at a psychiatric hospital, then released under the care of his therapist, Dr. Berger (Judd Hirsch).

For Beth, the perfectionistic mother (Mary Tyler Moore), Buck's drowning turns her well-ordered world completely upside down. She deals with the chaos quickly and efficiently by putting the family furniture back in place and restoring order to their social calendar. From all outward appearances, their home is back to normal, and Beth is back to her old self.

Her husband Calvin (Donald Sutherland) sees Beth's detachment from Conrad, who, if ever he needed a mother, needs one now. Calvin tries to bring them together, to bridge the chasm that is widening between them. But every attempt, however well-intentioned, is clumsy and ineffective, and he can only watch as his son's life unravels into a psychological mess.

Beth can't stand messes, which is why she can't get close enough to her son to help him. Beth is tidy. Everything in her home is meticulously kept, even the silverware, which waits in the dining-room drawer like a regiment of steadfast tin soldiers.

The movie is full of moments that will break your heart. Some of those moments are so real, so achingly real, that I wanted to jump into some of the scenes, shake the characters, and plead with them. "Stop all the fighting. Can't you see what you're doing? Talk to each other. Listen to each other. Help each other get through this. Don't walk away. Don't leave him out there by himself. He's your son, for God's sake. And he needs you."

Most of those things I wanted to say to Beth. Being a mother doesn't come easy to her, especially since the accident. There is a moment in the movie, though, when she tries to be the mother Conrad so desperately needs. It's a crisp autumn day as she looks out a sliding glass door to see him stretched out in a lounge chair in the backyard, his jacket draped over him. She opens the door and walks to where he is sitting.

"It's cold out here," she says, her words breaking the silence. "You should put that on, or you want a sweater?"

"Do I need one?"

"What are you doing?"

"Nothing. Thinking."

"About what?" she asks tentatively, as if putting a toe in the pool to test the water.

"Not about anything."

"Your hair is starting to grow out. It's looking better."

"I was thinking about the pigeon. You know, the one who used to hang around the garage and get on the top of your car and then take off when you pulled out of the driveway."

"Oh, yeah, I remember." And this brings a smile to her face. "I remember how scared I used to get when it would—WOOSH—every time I started the car."

"Yeah. That was the closest we ever came to having a pet."

It's just an observation he makes, not a criticism, but you can tell by her pause and the blink of her eyes that it's a reminder of one of her many failures as a mother. Watching her, you sense she is on the verge of detaching.

"You remember, Bucky asked you, he tried to talk you into getting a dog—"

As soon as he says "Bucky," Beth begins pulling out of the conversation, talking over Conrad's words, rattling on about the dog next door and how unfriendly a dog it was . . . and when Conrad barks abruptly, she stands up, breaking the connection.

"Put that on if you're going to stay out here, okay?"

After she goes inside, Conrad follows her. He finds her in the dining room, setting the table. He's not sure what he did to break the connection, but he's sure it was his fault. And he's sorry.

"Can I help?" he asks, trying to reestablish the connection.

"What, with this? No." Her words are cool and detached.

"I really want to." And in the way he says it, you can tell that Conrad is apologizing and begging for another chance all at the same time. But she misses the moment, as she has missed so many such moments in her son's life.

"What you can do is clean up that room of yours. It really is a mess, you know."

The phone rings and you feel the ache in Conrad's heart as she answers the phone, her words suddenly carefree and chatty.

The scene is an important one, because the story is about a family that can't connect. Three people living under the same roof, and they can't connect with one another in a way that allows them to talk about their loss. No one is able to touch the other or to be touched in return. They must bear their pain the best they can, and bear it alone.

I'm not sure how often the people living under my roof have tried to connect with one another but for some reason or another have failed. Too often, though, I'm sure of that. How many times have my children come up to me when they were little, saying, "Can I help?" And how many times did I answer, "What, with this? No. What you *can* do is clean up that room of yours. It really is a mess, you know."

The mess in Conrad's room is minor compared to the mess he has made of their conversation, or so it seems to him. Conrad was wanting to reestablish the connection with his mother that had been abruptly cut off in the backyard, though he is too emotionally inarticulate to be able to put that into words. Connection is something we all need and desperately long for, especially with the members of our family. Sadly, for whatever reason, it is often those we love most that we connect with least. Why? I wish I knew. And I wish I were better at it myself.

I make a mess out of my office, especially when a deadline is bearing down on me, and, if I could confine the mess to my office, it wouldn't be so bad. I haven't been able to do that very well. Especially with those I love most. I sometimes say too much, and, however neatly pressed the words, there really isn't room for them in the conversation, so they end up on the floor. I sometimes overreact, leaving words strewn about the floor like a month's worth of dirty clothes. And there are times I get so frustrated with my own messes that I project my frustration onto those around me.

In *Bird by Bird*, her book about writing and life, Anne Lamott wrote: "What people somehow (inadvertently, I'm sure) forgot to mention when we were children was that we need to make messes in order to find out who we are and why we are here—and, by extension, what we're supposed to be writing." [2]

By "messes," she's talking about more than the messes in a child's room. She's talking about relational messes, conversational messes, moral messes. Messes we all make. Messes we all *need* to make while we're still at home where someone there can help us work through them. How else can we find out who we really are and why we are really here? How else can we know mercy if we ourselves have not been in some kind of mess that required someone's mercy to get us out or to find our way through it? How else can we know love or grace or forgiveness, if not through all the messes in all the rooms that make up our life?

Conrad didn't go to his room to clean up his mess. When the phone rang, he just stood there, waiting, watching, listening. How many times, I wonder, have my children seen me pick up the phone, the way Beth did, and sound more glad to talk with the person on the other end than to talk with them? I was so oblivious to what they may have heard when I spoke to them, even more oblivious to how they felt about what I said. How alone that must have made them feel. And alone is not a good place for anyone, especially for a kid.

And especially for a kid like Conrad. Sometimes when he's alone, he has flashbacks of the night of the accident. And they bring everything back, the deafening roar of the wind, the numbing chill of the water, the fear, the darkness. Then the sound of Buck's voice, and the feel of his hand slipping away. Anything may trigger them. He never knows when they'll come or what terrible things he will do to himself when they do.

He doesn't need to be alone. He needs to connect. He knows that.

The sessions Conrad has with his therapist are escapes from his aloneness, but the connection, in spite of Dr. Berger's attempts, is tenuous. Conrad is not an easy person to connect with. The only person Conrad can talk with is a girl who was a fellow patient in the psychiatric hospital. The relationship seems good for him, holding out the hope that through it may come the beginning of his healing.

Until one day when he calls her.

And she isn't the one who picks up the phone. It's her father. She has committed suicide, he tells him. Conrad runs frantically to the bathroom and turns on the faucet to splash water in his face.

The water triggers a flashback.

He and Buck are in the water, arms across the hull of their capsized boat, holding on to each other as the rain lashes down at them and windswept waves crash over them. Conrad runs from the house, crying out: "Stay with me! Don't let go! Buck! Buck!"

The flashbacks keep coming, dogging his heels the faster he runs.

He comes to a phone booth and calls Dr. Berger, then runs to meet him at his office. The sounds of that fateful night get closer, louder. Out of breath and trembling with fear, Conrad bursts into Dr. Berger's office.

"Something happened. Something happened. Oh, God!" Conrad breaks down weeping. "I need something."

"What do you need?" asks Dr. Berger.

"It just keeps coming. I can't make it stop."

"Don't try."

"I've got to get off the hook for it. I've got to get off the hook."

"For what?"

"For what I did. For what I did to him."

"What did you do?"

"It's something, it's something, don't you see? It's got to be someone's fault . . . or there's no point."

"What point?" Berger says. "It happened."

Conrad breaks down, sobbing. "Bucky. I didn't mean it, Bucky. I didn't mean it. Bucky!"

"I know that," says Berger. "It wasn't your fault."

"But it was. You said 'get down the sail,' and I couldn't. I couldn't, and then the halyard, the halyard jammed. It jammed and then . . . and you . . . and you said I was supposed to take care of it. I was supposed to . . . "

"And that wasn't fair, was it?" Berger shoves the question in Conrad's face.

"No. And then you said, 'hang on, hang on.' And then you let go. Why'd you let go?"

"Because I got tired," Berger says, answering for Buck.

Conrad explodes at his deceased brother. "You jerk!" And his chest heaves in and out.

"It hurts to be mad at him, doesn't it?"

"Yep," Conrad answers, his anger easing. "He just wasn't careful. He just wasn't careful. He should see how a bad thing might happen."

"Bad things happen even when people are careful."

"We were out there . . . and we should've, we should've come in when it started to look bad."

"So you made a mistake."

"Why'd he let go? Why?"

"Maybe you were stronger. Did it ever occur to you that you might have been stronger?" Berger stops there and pauses, allowing the words to sink in. "How long are you going to punish yourself? When are you going to quit?"

"I'd like to quit."

"Why don't you?"

"It's not that easy. . . . I loved him."

"I know."

For a few minutes they talk about the suicide of Conrad's friend, and this brings a fresh wave of emotion. "Why do things have to happen to people? It isn't fair."

"You're right, life isn't fair."

"You do one wrong thing and—"

"And what was the one wrong thing you did?" Berger lets the question hang in the air until Conrad takes hold of it. "You know." Conrad does know, but it is hard for him to say. "You know."

"I hung on, stayed with the boat." And this triggers another flashback of him holding on to the boat.

"Now you can live with that, can't you?"

A final picture comes back to him, then it's over. "I'm scared."

"Feelings are scary and sometimes painful," counsels Berger. "If you can't feel pain, you can't feel anything else. Do you hear what I'm saying? You're alive and don't tell me you don't feel that."

"It doesn't feel good."

"It is good, believe me."

"How do you know?"

"Because I'm your friend."

"I don't know what I would have done if you hadn't of been here. You're really my friend?"

"I am, you can count on it."

Conrad falls sobbing into Dr. Berger's arms, and he stays in his arms a long time, holding on for dear life, because it is his dear life that has just been saved.

That is my favorite moment in the film, the moment when the storm subsides in Conrad's life. It seemed to me, as I reflected on it, a beautiful picture of the ministry of the Holy Spirit in our lives. He is the Counselor, the One called alongside to help us and comfort us, the way Dr. Berger came alongside Conrad. Dr. Berger listened. He asked questions. He made a few comments. But most of all, he was there.

We were not forgotten back there when we were hurt so badly, wounded so deeply, crushed so completely. The Holy Spirit is mindful of our hurts and faithful in healing them.

That's why the flashbacks come. Because it is our time to be healed.

The process is sometimes slow and most times painful. But the Holy Spirit is there for us. He will walk us through it, talk us through it, and most of all, love us through it.

Reflections on
Saving Private Ryan

For your tomorrow, they gave their today.

A quote on a stone near the Allied cemeteries in Normandy

I went by myself. My wife Judy didn't want to see it. Who could blame her? I was not totally unprepared for what I was about to see when I bought my ticket to *Saving Private Ryan*, but I was not totally prepared either.

The amphibious landing at Omaha Beach is the most riveting film-making I have ever seen. You couldn't bear to watch. But you couldn't bear not to watch either, because what you were watching was true. Much of it was filmed with hand-held cameras, giving the footage the feel of being shot by a newsreel cameraman.

The film opens serenely enough with an American flag waving in the wind, filling the entire screen. An older man walks ahead of his family through a military cemetery. Countless white crosses fill the cemetery like a regiment of soldiers standing at attention. He comes to the cross he was looking for and falls to his knees. His face is wrinkled, his lips are trembling, his eyes are glistening, as the memories of war come flooding over him.

Superimposed over this emotional image on the screen are the words:

June 6, 1994. Dog Green Sector, Omaha Beach.

The D-Day invasion was the largest amphibious assault in human history. And, the most pivotal.

The camera focuses on the hand of Captain John Miller, played by Tom Hanks, as it shakes trying to open his canteen. We can feel the spray of salt water as the front of the Higgins boat rises with a wave, then crashes hard against the water. Soldiers, loaded with gear, are packed in the boat, scared, shivering, and seasick.

"Thirty seconds!" signals Miller. "God be with you."

One of the soldiers makes the sign of the cross.

We then see the incoming armada of landing craft from the point of view of the German machine-gun nests. And you know, before a bullet is fired, that you are about to witness an unspeakable slaughter.

A whistle blows. The front of one of the Higgins boats drops open. As soon as it does, row after row of soldiers are shot like prisoners before a firing squad. We hear enemy bullets pinging against metal and ricocheting. Then the deafening noise of mortar fire.

The fronts of other boats open, sentencing other soldiers to the same fate. Some fall into water that is over their heads, and they sink under the weight of their backpacks. Some, unable to free themselves from their gear, drown. Others are hit by a barrage of stray bullets that zip through the water, and clouds of blood billow from the chests of dead soldiers.

Again, we see the carnage through the sights of German gunners. The men who make it to the beach are sprayed with a fusillade of bullets. The blood of U.S. infantrymen dyes the lapping surf.

Everything is bedlam and terror and noise. Mortars are exploding all around, potholing the beach and decimating the troops. Machine-gun fire is kicking up sand and ripping into the bodies of defenseless young men, scrambling for cover. We hear the screams of soldiers who have lost hands, arms, and legs.

There is no retreat. With the ocean behind them and the Germans ahead of them, there are only two options. Go forward or get killed.

In the disorienting chaos, medics try to staunch the pulsing wound of a fallen soldier. Before they can, a German bullet slams into his head. The frustration of the medics is excruciating to watch. Their efforts are futile. At best, they can buy only a few minutes of agony for the men they are so desperately trying to save.

The shelling goes on, relentlessly. The blistering gunfire, with its merciless indifference, rakes across the beach. You can see the chaos. You can hear the bullets whizzing by you. You can smell the smoke. Taste the fear.

A handful of men, under the command of Captain John Miller, storm a machine-gun nest that is fortified with concrete. They throw grenades into the bunker, then torch it with a flamethrower. The Germans that exit the bunker are in flames, and are immediately gunned down. Other Germans who surrender are executed by soldiers caught up in a frenzy of revenge.

One by one the German bunkers are destroyed. The beach is secured. It is a victory for the Americans, but a Pyrrhic one. The twenty-three-minute scene ends the way it began, with a close-up of Tom Hanks' hand, trembling as it tries to unscrew the top on his canteen.

There has never been a movie that captured the horror of war like this one. With gripping realism director Steven Spielberg puts us with the U.S.

troops that stormed Omaha Beach that fateful day in June. With them we feel the absolute terror of war, the panic of being hopelessly outgunned. With them we hear the deafening percussion of artillery shells exploding all around them, the rapid fire of machine-gun bullets tearing apart the bodies of eighteen-, nineteen-, twenty-year-old boys. With them we witness the unspeakable carnage of fellow soldiers strewn across the beach, their bodies blown apart, missing arms, missing legs, as the wounded writhe in the sand, staining it with their blood.

Spielberg talks about the story and why he was attracted to it: "The film is based on a number of true stories from the Second World War and even from the Civil War about brothers who have died in combat. Hanks leads a squad of men to retrieve the last surviving brother of four in order to send him back to his grieving mother in Iowa. Matt Damon plays Private Ryan. What first attracted me to the story was its obvious human interest. This was a mission of mercy, not the charge up San Juan Hill."[1]

After the rescue team finally finds Private Ryan, he won't leave his post, determined to stand beside the men who had now become as close as brothers. One of the soldiers dispatched to find Private Ryan was Sergeant Horvath, played by Tom Sizemore. Thinking out loud, he says to the rescue team: "I don't know, part of me thinks the kid is right. He asks what he's done to deserve this. He wants to stay here, fine. Let's leave him and go home. But then another part of me thinks, what if by some miracle we stay, then actually make it out of here. Someday we might look back on this and decide that saving Private Ryan was the one decent thing we were able to pull out of this whole God-awful mess. Like you said, Captain, maybe we do that, we all earn the right to go home."

Private Ryan's case was not an isolated one. Five brothers, for example, whose last name was Sullivan, were all in the Navy and all assigned to the same ship. When the ship came under enemy fire, it sank, taking all five brothers with it. Four Niland brothers—Edward (31), Dustin (29), Robert (25), and Chris (24)—all fought in the same fighter squadron, and they all died. You see the same sad stories etched on the gravestones of Civil War soldiers and those of World War I.

Anticipating that the movie would evoke a strong reaction from veterans and nonveterans alike, America Online set up a Web site where people could voice their feelings about the movie, and even talk with others who had seen the film. Over 30,000 responded. One said:

"When my friend and I went to see *Saving Private Ryan,* we expected to see another war film like all the others that we have seen. We are both teenagers and at one point had glorious visions of going into battle and defeating the evil Communists (or other) foe. After the first scene in this movie, our opinions of war changed." [2]

I have to say, from the horrible carnage on Omaha Beach, that my own opinions of war changed as well.

Another online comment: "I have never had a movie affect me as much as this one has. . . . For those of you who think war will solve our problems, watch this movie and picture your sons in the first thirty minutes." [3]

As I watched the movie, I did picture my son on that beach. He wants to be surgeon, so the part he would most probably be assigned would be the one of a medic. I pictured him on that beach with the shreds of a soldier's insides slipping through his hands, trying desperately to find the severed arteries so he can stop the bleeding. And I see the life go out of his face as he watches a boy, just out of high school, die in his arms. He would risk his life time and time again on that beach, running from one screaming soldier to another. And I don't know what would be a worse fate for him. To die on the beach. Or to live with the memories. But I do know this. If ever I would have to send *my* son to war, the fate of the world would have to be at stake, as it was in World War II, before I would allow him to go.

Another AOL subscriber said this: "Every family around the world should see this movie so that we will never forget the pain, the suffering, and the absolute horror that is war. Because every time someone forgets, another generation of young men dies and another field of white crosses is born."[4]

Another echoed that sentiment: "This movie should be shown along with *Born on the Fourth of July* in Congress and the Senate before young men are sent to war."[5]

A filmmaker could have directed the taking of Omaha Beach as a PG movie. But it would, at best, be a half-truth. At worst, an out-and-out a lie. And to what end? To make the movies a safe place for families? To protect the sensibilities of the audience? To gain a larger take of the box office since a milder rating would allow more people to see it?

Some movies aren't meant for families. Some movies are meant for fathers and mothers and politicians who vote to deploy U.S. troops around the world. Had this movie been shown at the outset of the Vietnam War, I think it could very well have prevented the war. And the film, though it had been graphic in its depiction of war, would have saved lives. Fifty-eight thousand American lives. Fifty-eight thousand sons and daughters could have been spared, if only a filmmaker had had the courage to tell the truth, and an audience had had the courage to listen.

Another AOL subscriber said this: "My father never told me about his WW II experiences until he was four days from death from cancer in 1992. He explained, in the same detail as *Saving Private Ryan*, the terrible truth about war and his experience in the Pacific theater.

"After seeing the movie, I know why he never wanted me to go to Vietnam.

"I love you, Dad." [6]

I grew up in the '50s, watching war movies starring John Wayne and loving it. I loved the suspense of war. The ambushes and the booby traps. Aircraft strafing ground troops. Bombs exploding everywhere. In my elementary school art class, I always drew war pictures, with things like squadrons of Flying Tigers swooping down on enemy tanks. My art teacher always gave me B's for them, and, if they were particularly bloody, C's. I remember the day she gave me an A. And I remember the picture I drew that softened her. It was a picture of a tree. An ordinary, boring, undramatic tree.

The kids in the neighborhood I grew up in played two kinds of army. "Big army" and "little army." "Big army" was when we played the soldiers ourselves, taking our plastic guns and shooting it out behind bushes and trash cans. "Little army" was when we built forts and used miniature army men to fight our battles. We would all have our favorite men, usually ones that could tumble well when a mortar blasted them into the air or when they dove for cover to dodge a spray of machine-gun bullets.

In the wars I fought and watched and drew, the good guys always won the day, no matter the odds against them. They may have gotten wounded, but they emerged as heroes. I felt that way until Vietnam. I was a senior in high school with a relatively low draft number, and though I planned to go to college, I felt torn. I had two cousins who had enlisted in the marines, and I thought that volunteering was the patriotic thing to do. Wouldn't the Duke have done the same? I thought that way until my father, who had fought in World War II, talked me out of it. When I saw *The Green Berets* with John Wayne and that patriotic theme song, I wasn't sure I had made the right decision. When I saw *Platoon,* I was.

Director Oliver Stone said that it was the John Wayne movie *The Sands of Iwo Jima,* with its romanticized version of war, that prompted his trip to Vietnam. That is why he had to make *Platoon.* To tell the truth about war.

"Innocence is the first casualty of war," is the way the posters read. After seeing the movie, I knew what the poster said was not the hype of some advertising executive. It was the truth. When the movie was over, my wife and I walked silently to our car. Once inside, we wept in each other's arms. We wept for the young boy who was our son, begging God not to have his innocence lost the way so many young men sent to Vietnam lost theirs.

There was a spate of Vietnam movies after *Platoon.* I saw none of them. In fact, I don't think I saw a war movie again until I saw *Saving Private Ryan.*

To confirm the truth of what I had seen that day on the screen, a friend of mine told me her experience when she saw *Saving Private Ryan.* When the movie was over, the audience sat in their seats, waiting for their tears to dry before they left the theater. As they sat in their rows, one by one they began turning their heads.

Two old men were standing in the back of the theater . . . saluting the screen.

Once again, the audience wept.

And if any of them doubted how true to life the film was, they doubted it no longer.

On a level different from the personal level represented by those e-mails, *Saving Private Ryan* is a graphic reminder of the reality of the spiritual battle that wages all around us.

In a charge that sounds like the ones Winston Churchill once gave to the British people, the Apostle Paul says: "Put on the full armor of God, that you may be able to stand firm against the schemes of the devil. For our struggle is not against flesh and blood, but against the rulers, against the powers, against the world forces of this darkness, against the spiritual forces of wickedness in the heavenly places. . . . In addition to all, taking up the shield of faith with which you will be able to extinguish all the flaming missiles of the evil one" (Ephesians 6:11-12, 16).

A.W. Tozer once said that life is not a playground, it is a battleground.

The territory that is being fought over is the human heart. Every day the battle rages. And every day a little bit of that territory is either gained or lost. Our Enemy is vigilant, waiting in his bunker with his guns loaded. As long as we're involved in trivial pursuits an ocean away, he's only too glad to leave us alone. But the moment we set foot on a beachhead that is his, he turns his sights on us, as the Germans did when the Higgins boats approached Omaha Beach. And he unleashes all the firepower at his disposal.

The spiritual war to which Paul refers to is real. The Enemy is real. The battle is real. The casualties are real. That is why our Lord instructed us to pray: "Do not lead us into temptation, but deliver us from evil" (Matthew 6:13).

For He, too, had once been led to such a beach (Matthew 4:1). And He knew that if we followed in His steps unprotected, we would end up casualties of war.

Just like the soldiers on Omaha Beach.

Reflections on *Smoke*

Annette Insdorf (interviewer): *I like the title of the film,* Smoke. *It's catchy and evocative. Would you care to elaborate?"*

Paul Auster (author/screenwriter): *On the word "smoke"? I'd say it's many things all at once. It refers to the cigar store, of course, but also to the way smoke can obscure things and make them illegible. Smoke is something that is never fixed, that is constantly changing shape. In the same way that the characters in the film keep changing as their lives intersect. Smoke signals . . . smoke screens . . . smoke drifting through air. In small ways and large ways, each character is continually changed by the other characters around him."*[1]

Interview, "The Making of Smoke"

When a precious gem is embedded in rock, its brilliance is obscured. But by extracting the gem and holding it up to the light, its brilliance shines. The same can be said for a brilliant moment in a movie. There is a moment like that in the movie *Smoke*.

First written as a short story in the op-ed section of *The New York Times*, then later adapted for the screen, *Smoke* is a finely textured film, something like a collection of episodic short stories, each titled with a different character's name. Two of the characters are Auggie (Harvey Keitel), the smoke shop owner, and Paul (William Hurt), the brooding neighborhood novelist who buys his cigarettes there. The moment in the movie that moved me most happened between these two men.

If you see the movie in a theater, the brilliance of that moment can get lost in the shuffle of images that follow it. But if you rent the video, extracting the scene from the film and holding it up to the light, it sparkles. It is as flawless and finely cut a scene as you will ever see. It's wonderfully written and equally wonderfully acted. And directed. And edited. And scored. Each time I view it, I see some glint of light that I missed in a previous viewing.

This rare moment begins in a smoke shop at the corner of Third Street and Seventh Avenue in Brooklyn, New York. The shop is the hub of daytime social life for many of the men in the area. For the few minutes it takes to have a smoke, they talk sports, air their gripes about the government, and put in their two cents' worth whenever they feel the collective wisdom in the shop is coming up a little short.

At the center of the hub is Auggie, who makes good conversation and a few dollars on the side by importing Cuban cigars. Paul, one of the regulars, sometimes raises the level of the conversations by contributing anecdotes on such things as the history of tobacco and who first calculated the weight of smoke, a concept he finds strange, "almost like weighing someone's soul." Like the first visible trace of smoke from a just-lit cigarette, those words introduce a spiritual theme that laces through the movie.

Paul doesn't hang around for much of the small talk though, not since his wife, Ellen, was killed by a stray bullet in a burglary that took place down the street. He lives in a small apartment, where he is kept company by a manual typewriter that hasn't been very companionable lately. He has written three or four novels on it, but has finished nothing since Ellen's death.

One evening Paul leaves that apartment, trying to make it to the smoke shop before it closes. When he gets there, he's out of breath but manages to catch Auggie just as he is walking out the door.

"You closed?"

"Run out of Schimmelpennincks?" asks Auggie, referring to Paul's brand of cigarettes.

"Suppose I could buy a couple off you before you leave?"

"No problem. It's not as though I'm rushing off to the opera or any-thing."

Once inside the darkened store, Auggie goes behind the counter to find Paul's cigarettes. As he does, something on the counter catches Paul's eye.

"Looks like someone forgot a camera."

"Yeah, I did."

"It's yours?"

"It's mine all right. I've owned that little sucker for a long time."

"I didn't know you took pictures," Paul says, mildly surprised.

"I guess you could call it a hobby. It only takes me five minutes a day to do it, but I do it every day. Rain or shine, sleet or snow. Sort of like the postman."

"So you're not just some guy who pushes coins across a counter."

"Well that's what people see, but . . . that ain't necessarily what I am."

Their conversation moves from the smoke shop to Auggie's apartment, where Paul is seated at a table, turning the pages of a photo album. From the looks of the empty bottles of beer and the stubs in the ashtray, they've been there awhile. Paul seems to be searching for words that will approxi-mate a compliment, but he's stumped, and all he can come up with is, "They're all the same."

"That's right," Auggie says proudly. "More than four thousand pictures of the same place. The corner of Third Street and Seventh Avenue at eight o'clock in the morning. Four thousand straight days in all kinds of weather. That's why I can never take a vacation. I've got to be in my spot every morning at the same time. Every morning in the same spot at the same time."

Amazed, Paul comments, "I've never seen anything like it."

"It's my project. What you'd call my life's work."

"Amazing. I'm not sure I get it though. I mean, what was it that gave you the idea to do this . . . project?

"I don't know, it just came to me. It's my corner, after all. I mean it's just one little part of the world, but things take place there too, just like everywhere else. It's a record of my little spot."

"It's kind of overwhelming," Paul says as he comes to the end of the album. As he does, Auggie plops another one in front of him. Paul turns the pages more quickly now, looking at them more out of politeness than genuine interest.

"You'll never get it if you don't slow down, my friend," Auggie says.

"What do you mean?"

"I mean, you're going too fast. You're hardly even looking at the pictures."

"But they're all the same."

"They're all the same, but each one is different from every other one. You've got your bright mornings and your dark mornings. You've got your summer light and your autumn light. You've got your weekdays and your weekends. You've got your people in overcoats and galoshes, and you've got your people in shorts and T-shirts. Sometimes the same people, sometimes different ones. And sometimes the different ones become the same, and the same ones disappear. The earth revolves around the sun, and every day the light from the sun hits the earth at a different angle."

"Slow down, huh?"

"That's what I'd recommend. You know how it is. 'Tomorrow and tomorrow and tomorrow, time creeps on its petty pace,'" Auggie says, quoting *Macbeth*.

Paul slows down and begins studying the pictures. The camera shows us several of them from his point of view, and they draw us into them. He looks at one page of pictures. And another. Then turning the page, he sees a picture that stops him. "Jesus. Look. It's Ellen."

"Yeah, that's her all right. She's in quite a few from that year. She must have been on her way to work."

Paul looks deeply into the photograph. "It's Ellen. Look at her. Look at my sweet darling." And he lingers over it until at last it overwhelms him. He starts to weep, and as he does, Auggie puts his arm around his shoulder.

The scene cuts to Auggie at eight the next morning, adjusting a camera that stands on a tripod across the corner from his store. He jots a note on a pad of paper, takes his picture, and captures another moment as a record of his little spot.

There are so many facets to this scene, and each throws off a little different angle of light. There's something beautiful, even spiritual, about two men communing over cigarettes, a few beers, and a stack of photo albums. It's not the television set they're glued to, it's a man's life's work. It's not Monday Night Football that captures their attention, it's art. They're not talking about superficial things, they're talking about sacred things.

Frederick Buechner once explained why he kept a record of his corner and why he shares that record with others through his books. Because the story of one of us, he writes, is in some way the story of all of us. For the one reading the account, he goes on to explain, it's like looking though someone else's photograph album. "What holds you, if nothing else, is the possibility that somewhere among all those shots of people you never knew and places you never saw, you may come across something or someone you recognize. In fact—for more curious things have happened—even in a stranger's album, there is always the possibility that as the pages flip by, on one of them you may even catch a glimpse of yourself. Even if both of those fail, there is still a third possibility which is perhaps the happiest of them all, and this is that once I have put away my album for good, you may in the privacy of your heart take out the album of your own life and search it for the people and places you have loved and learned from yourself, and for those moments in the past—many of them half forgotten—through which you glimpsed, however dimly and fleetingly, the sacredness of your own journey."[2]

The journey we are on is a sacred one. It is sacred because we are sacred. And we are sacred because we are the object of divine affection. It is the value God places on us that makes us sacred. Though on any given Monday it doesn't feel that way. It doesn't feel that way because we get caught up in a workaday routine that wears us down, and we lose a sense of the sacred in our work. Instead of living in the moment, we live for the weekends. And the moments which could be moments of grace become merely moments of clock-watching for the end of the day. In the gears of such a way of living, our humanity is ground down. And we forget how dear we are to God, how dear our neighbor is to God, and our mate, and our children.

I forget daily, and so I need to be reminded daily.

I need to be reminded that you, my neighbor whom God has called me to love, are not just some person who pushes coins across a counter. Just as I am not just some person who taps his fingers across a keyboard. You are not just some person who balances a budget, teaches a class, programs a computer, or whatever it is you do to make a living. You and I are unique. No one has ever existed who is quite like us. And when we're gone, no one will ever be able to quite fill the emptiness that our absence leaves behind.

You and I have been given a unique set of ears with which to hear, a unique set of eyes with which to see, and a unique heart with which to feel about all those things we have seen and heard.

God has put you on a corner of the world, just as He has put me. You have your corner. I have mine. It's just one little part of the world, but things take place there too, just like everywhere else. I can't begin to weigh what all has been lost in my life because I thought there wasn't anything taking place on the corner where God had placed me. So often I was looking down the street at some other corner where there seemed to be a lot going on. A lot of traffic in the streets, a lot of people on the sidewalks, a lot of noise in the air, a lot of activity everywhere. And it seemed to me, from where I was standing, that nothing was really happening on my corner. The truth is, a lot of things were taking place on my corner then and are taking place there still. Just as they are taking place on your corner too.

But if we don't slow down, we'll miss it.

God has put us on that corner to chronicle what takes place there. To chronicle it not as a hobbyist or a historian, but as a redeemer. He has put us on that corner not just to take pictures and be attentive to the pictures but to redeem the pictures. To bring color to a teenager who feels like a faded photograph, just another black-and-white face in a nameless crowd. To restore the soul of a man who has been worn down by life, who feels like a tattered, dog-eared photograph that no one has much use for anymore. To lift up the woman who has been stepped on by a lot of people who have passed her by, and dust off the footprints so others can see something of the sacredness of her life.

That is our life's work. To pay attention to those who pass by our corner. To see them the way Jesus would see them if He were standing on that corner. To hear them the way He would hear them. And to love them the way He would love them. To touch them with His hands, embrace them with His arms, and support them with His shoulder.

Then someday, when we leave this earth and are brought before the Judgment Seat of Christ, we will be able to give Him all of our photo albums. And we will be able to say to Him: "This is what we've done with the life You've given us. These are the people that we've laughed with and cried with and shared our lives with. These are the people who in Your name we loved, and in Your name we served. Though our lives were like smoke that was here today and gone tomorrow, it was sacred smoke.

"And for that brief moment on our corner, we thank You, Lord Jesus."

Reflections on *Hoosiers*

I was a sportswriter once for a couple of years in downstate Illinois. I covered mostly high school sports, and if I were a sportswriter again, I'd want to cover them again. There is a passion to high school sports that transcends anything that comes afterward; nothing in pro sports equals the intensity of a really important high school basketball game.[1]

ROGER EBERT

Film review of Hoosiers

Our enjoyment of movies is largely subjective. Depending on things as significant as our life experiences or as insignificant as the mood we were in when we saw it, our reaction to a movie can be a pendulum swing of emotions.

Take the movie *Stepmom*, for example, which stars Susan Sarandon and Julia Roberts. My wife and I saw it the first day it came out—Christmas. We both loved it, and in several parts of the movie we both cried.

A friend of ours thought it was so-so.

Another friend hated it. I mean *really* hated it. And for good reason. The television spot that advertised it the week before Christmas sold it as a comedy with the two actresses in a tug-of-war over the children. What the ad didn't tell you was that one of the actresses was dying of cancer. So if you went to the movies on Christmas, expecting something lighthearted like *Home Alone*, you would be disappointed, maybe even angered, as my friend was. Cancer runs in her family, and she has had a scare with it herself. In light of her life experiences it's easy to understand her reaction.

Because of my own life experiences, *Hoosiers* is one of my favorite films. I took my oldest daughter with me when I first saw it, expecting little more than a movie with lots of basketball.

The musical score starts with one slender melodic thread. From there the note is so seamlessly woven into the fabric of the story that you can't imagine the film without it. Over the film score and opening credits, the camera follows an old gray car across the Indiana countryside. Gene Hackman, the new coach, is driving. It's a long drive; part of it takes place at night. Then at dawn, passing golden fields and an old barn where kids are shooting baskets, he arrives in town, stopping in front of Hickory High School.

Right then, in the first minute of the movie, my body trembled, my chest started to heave. I did everything to hold back the tears, but everything wasn't enough. Off and on through the entire movie I cried. That has never happened to me at a movie. Ever. As I cried, my oldest daughter tenderly put her hand on my arm, petting it to console me, unaware of what was behind those sudden tears.

Three things were behind those tears.

One of them was my father, who had passed away three years earlier. He had come to a small town like the one in the movie, where he started his career as a high school football coach. He drove there in an old gray car like the one in the movie, which he had named "the Gray Goose." For a moment, that old gray car brought him back to me. Suddenly, unexpectedly, I felt the full weight of that loss. And I could hardly bear it.

The second reason for those sudden tears was that I had been working on a screenplay about my father's first year as a coach. My opening scene had my dad and mom driving cross-country in an old gray car to the small town of McKinney, Texas, a town much like the one in the movie.

While I was working on the screenplay, the boys who had played for him from 1946 to 1948 hosted a forty-year reunion. They came from all over the country. They came to see a few friends, tell a few stories, touch a few memories. But most of all they came for Coach, to honor him, and to tell him how much he had meant to them. The next year he died.

Growing up, I had heard him tell a number of stories about those years. When I attended the reunion, I heard the players telling their own stories. It was then I realized what a special time it had been for each of them. For some of them it was a sacred time, a time that forever changed their lives.

The third reason behind those tears was that I had played high school basketball too. I went through some of the same drills the Hickory High team had gone through. I felt the same fear that Ollie had felt. I knew what it was like to be benched and experience a coach's scorn. I felt the embarrassment of their losses. And the exultation of their victories.

Three things I loved—my father, screenwriting, and basketball—all intersected that day at the movies.

Hoosiers is a story about the triumph of underdogs. One of them is Norman Dale (Gene Hackman), who had been forever barred from coaching college ball because of a punch he had thrown at one of his own players. This is his last chance. And the odds are stacked against him. At first the players don't like him. And the townspeople actively oppose him. Another underdog is Myra Fleener (Barbara Hershey), who returns to Hickory after her father dies in order to help her mother with the family business, giving up both her education and any chances of marrying. Still another underdog is Shooter (Dennis Hopper), an alcoholic who not only has lost his self-respect but the respect of his son, who plays on the team. And then there is Ollie, the shortest boy on the team, who thinks he's not tall enough or good enough to play.

The Saturday I was working on this chapter, I was also watching a basketball game on TV. Duke versus North Carolina State. In the waning minutes of the game, Duke was ahead by five points. During a time-out, when the station went to a commercial, I flipped through the remote to see what else was on.

Ironically, *Hoosiers* was on one of the channels.

The scene I tuned in on was the one where Hickory was playing in the regional finals. Ollie, the boy who thought he didn't count because he was too short and not any good, shot two free throws in the final seconds to win the game. In the matter of only a few seconds, tears pooled in my eyes. That happens every time I see the movie. I mean, *every* time. I've seen it ten, maybe twelve times, and though I know the story backwards and forwards, I always cry. I know every scene in the movie where I'm likely to cry, and *still* I cry.

I can say that about no other movie I have ever seen. But I can say this. The feelings run so deep that only this movie could touch them. Why, I can't tell you. All I can tell you is this. Art evokes feelings that often defy rational explanation, touching us, though we can't exactly explain why.

Maybe that is because art isn't, and was never meant to be, exact. That is both its beauty and its mystery.

I turned back to the Duke-N.C. State game until it was over. Then I turned back to *Hoosiers*. The team had just gotten off the bus to Indianapolis for the state championship. As they enter Butler Gymnasium, which seats 15,000, the boys are awestruck at its size. Seeing this, and fearing the effect it might have on the team's confidence, the coach takes out a tape measure and says, "Buddy, hold this under the backboard." The boy takes off his hard-sole shoes and walks onto the court.

It is a small detail, but anyone who's ever played basketball realizes its authenticity. When I played, we could only step onto our gym floor in our tennis shoes or in our socks. One reason for that was to keep from damaging the wood flooring. Another reason, I think, was out of a sense of reverence, for that rectangle of wood was holy ground, or at least as close to holy ground as a teenage boy was likely to get.

Buddy takes one end of the tape measure and the coach takes the other end, measuring off the distance between the backboard and the free-throw line.

"How much is it?" the coach asks.

"Fifteen feet," Buddy answers.

"Strap, put Ollie on your shoulder," says the coach, and they measure off the distance from the rim to the floor. "What's it say?"

"Ten feet."

"The exact same measurements as our gym in Hickory," observes the coach. And in that moment, the cavernous gym is brought down to the size of their own.

In the locker room before the game, Coach Dale says: "We're way past big speech time. I want to thank you for the last few months. They've been very special to me. Anybody have anything you want to say?"

One of the players says: "Let's win this one for all the small schools who never got a chance to get here."

Another player, Shooter's son, says: "I want to win for my dad."

Another player says: "Let's win for Coach, who got us here."

The minister and his assistant enter the locker room to give a blessing. The minister says, "With God of heaven, all is one—to deliver with a great multitude or a small company. For the victory of battle comes not from the multitude of hosts but the strength of heaven."

Then his assistant adds: "And David put his hand in the bag, and pulled out a stone and slung it, and it struck the Philistine in the head, and he fell to the ground. Amen."

It is a reverent scene, and even the coach shows his respect by joining his players who have their heads bowed in prayer. The scene ends with the coach and his players stacking their hands one on top of the other, with the coach saying four final words that will resonate in them for the rest of their lives.

"I love you guys."

When they break the circle, the scene jumps to courtside. Flashbulbs are going off everywhere as this David and Goliath matchup gets underway. In the early minutes of the game, Hickory, a school of 64, is getting trounced by South Bend Central, a school of 2,800 that had won last year's state championship. South Bend leads 16-6 when Coach Dale calls the first time-out. As the boys catch their breath on the bench, the coach says loudly over the roar of the crowd. "Maybe they were right about us. Maybe we *don't* belong up here." Those two, short sentences, along with a change in strategy, shifts the momentum.

Throughout the rest of the game the two teams exchange baskets. David gets close to the giant and takes a stone from his pouch.

In the last two minutes the score is Hickory 34, South Bend 40.

With 1:18 on the clock, the score is Hickory 36, South Bend 40.

With 33 seconds left, the scoreboard reads Hickory 38, South Bend 40.

With 25 seconds left, Jimmy Chitwood, probably the best player in the entire state, scores a layup, tying the score, 40 to 40.

The roar of the crowd is deafening. Then, when Hickory gets the ball, they call a time-out. As the coach dictates the last play, which uses Jimmy as a decoy and lets another one of the other boys shoot the final shot, the faces of the team members register a silent protest.

"What's wrong with you guys?" Coach Dale asks. But the boys remain silent. "What's the matter with you?"

The boys remain silent. Jimmy looks at them, then at the coach, and says, "I'll make it."

In the first half of the film, the coach wouldn't tolerate so much as a suggestion from his players, benching them before they even finished their thought. Here we see the final beat of the coach's character arc. He listens to his players and abandons his strategy, because he knows theirs is better.

As the clock winds down, Chitwood gets the ball, holding it until only five seconds remain. We see him in the foreground at the same time we see the scoreboard in the background. With the clock ticking down, Jimmy makes his move. He fakes one way—four seconds left—then goes the other—three seconds. He gets a step on his defender, and takes a jump shot at the top of the key. The moment is drawn out dramatically as the ball is tracked from four different camera angles. In the final second, the ball swishes through the net, making the Hickory Huskers the 1952 Indiana State Champions.

The film is a deeply religious one.

At the heart of the film is the theme of redemption. This is a story of second chances. "Give him a chance," Myra says at a town meeting where a vote has been called to dismiss the coach.

"When's the last time anyone's given him a chance?" the coach asks Shooter's son.

It's a second chance to coach for a man who had made a potentially career-ending mistake. It's a second chance for an alcoholic to make something of himself. And it's a second chance for him and his son to have a relationship. A second chance for Ollie, the boy apparently without the physique and talent to succeed. A second chance for the whole team, for that matter, which had gotten off to such a bad start without Jimmy Chitwood. A second chance for Myra too, who had seemingly given up so much when she came back to Hickory.

Some of what we feel about the movie is the unspoken hope that if there is a second chance for them, maybe, just maybe, there might be a second chance for us as well. God knows, in some area of our lives, we all need one.

Film is an emotional medium. This film is unembarrassingly so. To disregard the emotional element is like describing a human being only in terms of biology without taking into account psychology. A human being is both body and soul. To describe a person only in terms of physical characteristics is a critique. It may tell the truth, as far as it goes, but it doesn't tell the whole truth. For how do you describe love in purely biological terms? We can do that with sex, but not with love. Or hope. Or faith. The very things that separate us from the animal kingdom and help define our humanity.

I'm not sure where *Hoosiers* fits, if at all, on the American Film Institute's top 100 movies of all time. I'm not sure where it fits on your list. But on mine, the film is definitely in my top five and might very well be my favorite. It's a subjective choice, I realize that. It's one that is influenced by my life experiences and the emotions that are tied to those experiences. I can't explain a lot of the reasons why. All I know is that it touched me in places I didn't know even were there, let alone that needed touching.

But isn't that what art is supposed to do?

Reflections on *Hoop Dreams*

A film like Hoop Dreams *is what the movies are for. It takes us, shakes us,
and makes us think in new ways about the world around us.*[1]

ROGER EBERT

From his film review on Hoop Dreams

With an initial budget of $2,500, Steve James and Frederick Marx
started a documentary about basketball in the inner city. They started what they thought would be a six-day shoot. Eight years later they finished the shoot, $150,000 in debt. Originally the filmmakers hoped their
short documentary would be aired to a PBS audience. It ended up being
shown at movie theaters across the country, grossing $9 million and receiv-
ing numerous awards.

The filmmakers shot over 250 hours of film. The rough cut was eight
hours. The final edit brought the running time down to about 1 percent of
their total footage, 165 minutes to be exact. The film focuses on two four-
teen-year-olds in Chicago's inner city, William Gates and Arthur Agee, following them for the next four years until they graduate from high school.

The documentary is less about basketball and more about the inner city.
The camera takes us places the average middle-class white would never dare
to go. It shows us the poverty, the back-alley drug dealings, the pickup

games on cracked asphalt courts with weathered backboards and netless hoops. It takes us into the Cabrini Green housing project, William's neighborhood. It also takes us a few miles away to Arthur's neighborhood. And it shows the almost hopeless levels of impoverishment of those who live there.

But that is not all the camera shows us. It also shows the faith of black families, the courage of the mothers, the regrets of the fathers, the hopes and dreams of their sons, whose only ticket out of the ghetto is basketball.

"Right now, I want to play in the NBA. That's something I dream—think about all the time, playing in the NBA," says William Gates at the beginning of the documentary.

"When I get into the NBA, first thing I'm gonna do, I'm gonna see my momma. I'm gonna buy her a house. Gonna get my dad a Cadillac Oldsmobile so he can cruise to the games," says Arthur Agee.

These are their hoop dreams. The dream of getting out of the ghetto. The dream of doing something with their lives. The dream of giving their parents a better life. There is such—what's the right word?—such nobility to their dreams. And all through the documentary we are cheering for them, hoping their dreams do come true.

In an interview, Peter Gilbert, one of the producers of *Hoop Dreams,* had this to say about William and Arthur's dream: "If you grow up white and middle-class and you have the dream of being a basketball player, it's a dream with a safety net. We tried to show what it was like to have a dream with no safety net. Arthur and William are always on the edge of falling off. And it never ends for them. Even if they graduate from college, they're more on the edge than the average white, middle-class person would be."[2]

Even the homes they come from were on the edge. "Our lights were cut off," said Arthur's mom, "our gas was cut off, and we were sitting in the dark." And they sat in the dark, day in, day out, for three whole months. The only light came from a lamp that was connected to a long extension cord that was plugged into a wall socket of the downstairs apartment.

Can any of us imagine what that is like? No warm showers. No hot meals. No way to keep food in the refrigerator. No way to use the washing machine. Nothing. Nothing but one solitary lamp.

There are other levels of poverty in those neighborhoods besides the material kind. Many of the wives live without husbands. Many of the kids live without fathers. William's father has been completely absent from his life. Arthur's father has been in and out of his life, largely due to his addictions and his time in jail.

Absent from home for seven months, Arthur's dad has been in jail on a burglary charge. During that time, though, he overcame his crack cocaine addiction, and he renewed his faith in God. "While I was incarcerated," he says, "I just asked God, 'Show me a different way. Give me a new life. Take the taste of drugs and evil way of thinking away from me.' I asked the Lord to forgive me for what I did—the times that I mistreated my wife, beat her physically, you know. I just hope this be a lesson to my children to see me turn my life over to the Lord."

The moment in the documentary that emotionally grabbed me was the scene of Arthur's eighteenth birthday. His mother has made him a special birthday dinner with German chocolate cake, his favorite. "I want to show him how much we appreciate him and love him and care for him. Everything you can imagine was going wrong with this family, but now everybody's together." For a moment in their family's history, everybody is happy. And proud. "He's a great kid," Mrs. Agee says. Then suddenly the mood of the scene turns serious as she remarks, "And some kids don't even live to get this age, you know." But then her spirits lift again: "That's another thing to be proud of. It's his eighteenth birthday, he lived, and to get to see eighteen—that's good!"

The matter-of-fact way she said what she did astounded me almost as much as what she said. "It's his eighteenth birthday, he lived, and to get to see eighteen—that's good!" In all my life I've never had a thought like that about any of my children.

I have two who just turned eighteen. To celebrate, they wanted to have a party and invite their senior class. Not as overwhelming as it sounds. Their class is only a hundred, and we expected only half of them to show up. We went in with two other families—who also had eighteen-year-olds who were also celebrating their birthdays—and we rented the Palmer Lake Town Hall. Each family brought snacks and soft drinks.

We didn't worry about the kids who were coming. They came from a good Christian school, from good Christian homes, with good Christian parents. We didn't worry about drugs or alcohol. We didn't worry about gangs or drive-by shootings. All we worried about was how long the snacks would hold out and how well the stereo system would work.

"It's his eighteenth birthday, he lived, and to get to see eighteen—that's good!"

A moment like that follows you out of the theater. And with a haunting echo it calls to you. "Look at all you've been given," it says. "Be grateful." It also says, "Look beyond the safe, sequestered neighbor where you live. And see something, feel something, do something about those neighborhoods where mothers give thanks that their children have lived to see their eighteenth birthday."

During the LA riots, a Jewish radio talk-show host named Dennis Prager was a voice of sanity during an insane time in that city's history. One of the programs he had instituted brought together people of different races and different religious beliefs. He felt that if you invited strangers into your home whose views or life experiences were different than yours, and if they invited you into their home, it would help bridge the chasm between the two groups. We did that with one black family. They spent an evening with us. We spent an evening with them. Both of us were Christians, and they invited us to their church. I had never been to a black church before. It's a part of the black experience that you never see on the evening news. You never see the deep religious faith, the strong sense of community, the abiding hope in the midst of seemingly hopeless circumstances. At the end of the service they had an altar call. A gang member came forward and told his story, which was punctuated with "amens" and "praise the Lords" and "hallelujahs." When he was finished, he gave his life to Christ. It was a view into the black experience, and even that small view gave us a whole new understanding of their lives, their struggles, their hopes, their dreams.

That is also what *Hoop Dreams* did. It brought me into a neighborhood that I normally would have taken a detour around.

In the documentary I learned that William had fathered a child when he was fifteen. I didn't know why until I was doing some research on the Internet and discovered that a *Hoop Dreams* reunion had been held, bringing back the filmmakers and the two families they followed. "At that particular time," said William, "everybody in our neighborhood was getting killed

. . . everybody was dying. I thought that if something happened to me, I need to leave something behind to say I was here."

Does that not break your heart, that a fifteen-year-old boy, especially one living in the United States in the second half of the twentieth century, would have to grow up in such an environment, thinking those things, fearing those things?

During their high school years, William and Arthur were watched by college scouts, and later went to a basketball camp where they and premier ballplayers from all over the country were watched by major college coaches. The atmosphere was one of a meat market with some coaches looking for point guards, others looking for power forwards. The boys were commodities, that much was clear. And though to some extent we all are judged not by who we are but by what we can contribute, something about the process felt uncomfortable to watch.

High school for the boys had its ups and downs, both personally and athletically. William tore up his knee, and, in his coach's eyes, never lived up to his potential. Arthur never quite gained the star status to attract Division I interest. But both boys graduated. And both received basketball scholarships. Arthur would be leaving for Mineral Area Junior College. William was bound for a Division I college, Marquette. The day they each left home was an emotional one.

Arthur's coach arrives at the boy's home to drive him to the athletic housing at Mineral Area Junior College. Arthur's family forms a circle and joins hands as his father prays. "God, we thank you for this day, Lord. And we ask you to go with Junior, Lord. Go with him as he tries to better his education, Lord. And we thank you for coming this far, Lord. We came this far by faith, Lord. And we ask you, Father, when he get in college, Lord, to keep him, Lord, keep him protected. We thank you for him, Jesus. In Jesus' name we pray. Amen."

The whole family echoes his "Amen." As Arthur follows the coach down the steps of his house, he turns to his mother, and in the tenderest of moments, he wraps his arms around her. In her embrace he weeps. His mother had always been there for him, encouraging him in his dreams, pointing him in the right direction, loving him every step of the way. Now it's time for him to leave and for her to let go. With tears in their eyes, he breaks the embrace and leaves.

Not far from there another good-bye is taking place. Another basketball player from Marquette has come to pick up William. He, too, cries as he hugs his mother. "I'll miss you," she says.

"I'll miss you too."

And as they walk to the car, she gives him a few final words before she sends him on his way. "I want you to be good, okay? Don't get mixed up in trouble. Don't get no alcohol, no wine coolers, none of that stuff."

William nods and gives her a final hug before he leaves. She waves good-bye and watches until the car disappears. She walks back to her apartment, and you feel the mingling of emotions within her. She stands on the porch, alone. In a pensive moment she says, "I just hope he stays in there. That's what worries me most. Once he gets in the door, I want him to stay in there for four years." And in a low voice she adds, "I think he gonna make it, Lord, I hope so anyway."

After the two boys said their good-byes, I realized: Their story isn't just about *their* dreams. Their story is also about the dreams of their mothers, their fathers, their brothers and sisters, the dreams of all their extended families, dreams of the neighbors too. It is so beautiful and so heartrending at the same time. As I sat in the theater, it also became my dream for them. And my tears for them. And my prayers.

Toward the end of the documentary, William, now eighteen, says: "Four years ago, all I used to dream about was playing in the NBA. I don't really dream about it like that anymore. You know, even though I love basketball, I want to do other things with my life too. If I had to stop playing basketball right now, I think I'd still be happy. That's why when somebody say, 'When you get to the NBA, don't forget about me,' and all that stuff, I should say to them, 'Well, if I don't make it—what, you gonna forget about me?'"

Arthur's sentiments at eighteen are similar: "When I was young, when I was little, that's all I used to think about—the NBA. If I set my mind I can go. Get into a good college. I can go. But if I don't, I ain't gonna be no drug dealer, you know—cry about it, come back and stick up a gas station or nothing like that, you know. Probably go into comedy or architecture, something like that."

As I am typing this, I have *Hoosiers* playing on the VCR only a couple of feet away—what is that, thirteen times now?—and this team of underdogs just shot the winning basket against the odds-on favorite from a school that is forty-three times its size. With a swish of the net, their wildest dreams have come true. Indiana State Champions. Every one of the Hickory fans is going nuts. The music reaches a triumphant crescendo. And the fans are now streaming onto the court to embrace their hometown heroes. It's a deeply emotional moment. And it seems only right that this team that had worked so hard and overcame so much should walk away with the victory.

Then I think about these two wonderfully talented basketball players from the inner city, who also worked so hard, who also overcame so much, and my heart breaks. Reality has taken the air out of their once-buoyant dreams. Not all the air. But enough to where you can see the deflation in their eyes, hear it in their voices. You wish you could write the script that would put them in the NBA and their mothers in beautiful homes and their dads in nice cars. But you can't.

Arthur went on to play basketball at Arkansas State University, where he started as point guard his junior year. William ended up dropping out of basketball for a while in order to spend more time with his wife and daughter.

Each of the boys overcame almost insurmountable odds to follow their dream. William, who transferred to Saint Joseph's High School, overcame the poverty of the ghetto and learned how to adjust to life in a predominately white school. He overcame the obstacle of having a baby at fifteen and became a good father. He overcame two knee operations. He overcame all of that and received a scholarship at Marquette. He even overcame the university officials and succeeded in gaining approval to bring his wife and child there. He graduated with a communications major. His dream never took him to the NBA, but it took him out of the ghetto. And it took him to a lot of wonderful places along the way.

Director Steve James spoke about the deep desire each boy had to leave the violence and despair of the inner city. "The dream is about far more than the fantasy of playing in the NBA. It provides kids like William and Arthur with an identity and real opportunities. It can be a daily escape from the hard realities of the inner city and even help hold their families together. If they risk tragedy by caring too much about basketball, it's because the game is one of the precious few ways they know of to achieve a better life."[3]

William Gates now lives in Milwaukee with his wife and two children. Arthur lives in his old neighborhood with his wife and their two children. William is pursuing a career in marketing, public relations, or broadcasting. Arthur has been active as a public speaker and an actor. He has acted in such projects as *He Got Game* and the TNT original movie *Passing Glory*. He has also acted in commercials for Kodak and McDonald's. In addition to that, he has set up "The Arthur Agee Role Model Foundation," which believes that parents are the single most important influence in their children's lives, and he is committed to helping children achieve their goals and to go on to be positive role models.

When the documentary came out, Siskel and Ebert felt it was the best film of the year. Not best documentary. Best film. I remember hearing them say that, and at the time thinking it was an exaggeration.

Then I saw the film.

Were it not for that film, I would have never gone into William and Arthur's neighborhood. If I hadn't gone, I never would have seen my neighbors. And if I never see them, how in the world can I ever even *begin* to love them?

Reflections on
The Elephant Man

*The Elephant Man is a very pleasurable surprise. Though I had seen
Eraserhead, which is the only other feature directed by David Lynch, and had
thought him a true original, I wasn't prepared for the strength he would bring
out of understatement. . . . This young director (he's thirty-four) has extraordinary taste; it's not the kind of taste that enervates artists—it's closer to grace.*[1]

PAULINE KAEL

Former film critic for the New Yorker *from her review on* The Elephant Man

Pauline Kael spent her career writing movie reviews for the *New Yorker*
magazine. I have never read anyone who could critique a movie on as
many different levels as she can. She has a discriminating eye, a keen mind,
and an acerbic wit. Although I sometimes disagree with her, I have learned
much from her and have enjoyed learning it. She's a really good writer. That
being said, if I ever made a film, I would want to make sure it was released
when she was on vacation, preferably a long vacation in some really remote
part of the world that didn't have a movie theater. As a critic, she overlooks
nothing. She also likes nothing, at least that's the impression you get when
reading her. For example:

When Pulitzer Prize–winning columnist George Will reviewed *Shoah*, a nine-and-a-half-hour documentary based mostly on interviews of Holocaust survivors, he said this: "There has never been anything like it, or its subject, so there is something flat about saying that Shoah is the finest film ever. So say this: It is the noblest use to which cinema—the technology, the techniques—has been put, ever." 2

When Pauline Kael reviewed it, she called it "a long moan." 3

Here are a few more examples.

"*Out of Africa* dribbles on—adult, diligently cryptic, unsatisfying." 4

"*Top Gun* is a recruiting poster that isn't concerned with recruiting but with being a poster." 5

"I hope *Chariots of Fire* wasn't dedicated, like Liddell's sprinting, to the glory of God, because it looks as if it were thrown together in desperation in the cutting room." 6

Not a critic who is exactly philanthropic with her praise. Which is why her review of *The Elephant Man* caught my attention. Here are some of her comments.

"The grace in Lynch's work comes from care and thought: this is a film about the exhibition and exploitation of a freak, and he must be determined not to be an exploiter himself. The monster is covered or shadowed from us in the early sequences and we see only parts of him, a little at a time. Lynch builds up our interest in seeing more in a way that seems very natural. When we're ready to see him clearly, we do. By then, we have become so sympathetic that there's no disgust about seeing his full deformity. . . .

"Lynch holds you in scenes with almost no action: Merrick may be alone on the screen preening, or fondling the brushes and buffers in his gentleman's dressing case, or just laying them out in an orderly pattern and waltzing around them, like a swell, and you feel fixated, in a trance. . . .

"John Gielgud is in strapping form as the head of the hospital, and Wendy Hiller, as the chief nurse, matches him in vinegary elegance, syllable for syllable, pause for pause. John Hurt and Anthony Hopkins—both specialists in masochism—might have leaked so much emotion that the film would slip its sprockets. But Hopkins comes through with an unexpectedly crisp, highly varied performance—the kind you respect an actor for. . . .

"This is not the usual movie—in which the story supports the images and holds everything together. Lynch's visual scheme is so imaginative that it transcends the by now well-known story, and scene by scene you don't know what to expect. You're seeing something new—subconscious material stirring within the format of conventional narrative." [7]

If you haven't seen the film, it's based on the true story of a sideshow attraction billed as "The Elephant Man." This massively disfigured man lived in the late 1800s in England at the sooty, smoke-stacked height of the Industrial Revolution. His name was John Merrick (played by John Hurt in the film). He suffered from neurofibromatosis, a condition that caused tumors to grow all over his body, under his skin, around his nerves, even in his bones. After Merrick's death at age 27, plaster casts were made of his body, and his skeleton was preserved for future study, so what you see in the movie is how he really looked. Dr. Frederick Treves (Anthony Hopkins) was the physician who treated him, befriended him, and later wrote of him in a book titled *The Elephant Man and Other Reminiscences.*

I first saw the movie with my wife when I was a young pastor, fresh out of seminary. We were both deeply touched and had tears in our eyes when the movie ended. In fact, the whole theater was sniffing back tears. During the final credits, nobody got out of their seats. Even after the credits ended and the house lights came on, people were slow in getting up. No one talked. No one squeezed past you or crowded the aisles. If you were slow getting up, people were patient to wait. They understood. It were almost as if something of the sacredness of this man's life spilled onto the audience.

The film was a moving experience. Two of the moments in the film particularly moved me. One was the ending. The other was this moment.

The scene begins with Dr. Treves walking down the hall to bring a saucer of food to the Elephant Man, whom he has hidden in a small, upstairs room near the clock tower of the hospital. The head of the hospital, Mr. Carr-Gomm (John Gielgud), stops Treves and questions him. Why wasn't the patient properly admitted? Why is he in isolation? Is he contagious? And then the final, insurmountable question: Is he ultimately incurable? When Treves says yes, Carr-Gomm reminds him that there are places for incurables but his hospital isn't one of them. Treves knows the only way to keep him there is to convince Carr-Gomm that the Elephant Man is indeed a man and not a beast.

Later when Treves is alone with his patient, he makes his first serious attempt to communicate.

"I can't help you unless you help me. I believe you have something to tell me. Do you understand me? Just nod your head if you do. I want to hear you say it. Very slowly, I want you to say yes. Say yes."

Merrick slurps something sounding like a yes.

"Say: Hello, my name is—"

"Hello," Merrick struggles to say, "my name is—"

"John Merrick."

"John Merrick."

Treves is encouraged by the progress, but when Carr-Gomm tells him that he wants to meet this Mr. Merrick, the doctor knows that Merrick needs more time to rehearse. He suggests the meeting take place in a few days. Carr-Gomm says tomorrow at two o'clock. Not much time for all he has to teach Merrick. Treves starts by helping Merrick memorize a few lines out of the Twenty-third Psalm, and rehearsing with him a few of the answers to the questions he anticipates Carr-Gomm will ask.

"When I introduce you, say the words you've learned."

"Hello. My name is John Merrick. I'm very pleased to meet you."

At two o'clock, Carr-Gomm comes for his meeting. Treves brings the two of them together.

"John, may I introduce you to Mr. Carr-Gomm. Mr. Carr-Gomm, this is John Merrick."

"Hello. My name is John Merrick. I am very pleased to meet you."

"How are you feeling today?" asks Carr-Gomm.

"I feel much better."

"Are you comfortable here?"

"Everybody has been very kind."

"How is your bronchitis?"

This question seems to stump him. You hear the phlegmy sound of his breathing as he tries to come up with an answer. He looks at Dr. Treves, who rescues him with one of the questions they have rehearsed.

"Mr. Merrick likes the food here, don't you?"

"Much better than what I'm used to."

"I understand you've been flogged," says Carr-Gomm.

"I feel much better now."

"How do you find, Mr. Treves, I mean, as a teacher?"

Merrick searches for the words. "He's been very kind."

By now, Carr-Gomm is onto them. "How long did you and Mr. Treves prepare for this interview?"

"He's very kind," Merrick says.

"Of course, I understand. It's been a pleasure to meet you, Mr. Merrick. Good day to you."

As Carr-Gomm leaves the room, Treves follows him. Left in the room alone, Merrick starts reciting the lines of the psalm that Treves had rehearsed with him.

"The Lord is my shepherd; I shall not want. He maketh me to lie down in green pastures."

Outside the room, Carr-Gomm says, "It would have been a brave attempt, Mr. Treves, but the man was obviously simply mouthing the words taught by you."

"Yes, well, I'm sorry to have wasted your time."

Merrick's words filter through the door. "He restoreth my soul."

"He simply doesn't belong here," says Carr-Gomm. "He would be much better somewhere else where he could be constantly looked after. I'm sorry. Good day to you." Carr-Gomm turns and starts down the stairs, leaving Treves alone with his thoughts and the sound of Merrick's recitations that filter through the door. Then something in Merrick's words catches his attention.

"Yea, though I walk through the valley of the shadow of death, I will fear no—"

"Mr. Carr-Gomm!" Treves calls. Carr-Gomm comes back. "I didn't teach him that part," Treves says, rushing into the room with Carr-Gomm behind him.

"And I will dwell in the house of the Lord forever."

"How did you know the rest of it? I didn't teach you the rest of it."

"Very strange," remarks Carr-Gomm.

"How did you know the rest of it, the Twenty-third Psalm?"

"I used to read the Bible every day. I know it very well. And the Twenty-third Psalm is my favorite."

"Treves, come and see me in my office," says Carr-Gomm, leaving the two of them in the room.

"Why didn't you tell me you could read?"

"I was afraid to talk. Please forgive me."

Once Treves joins Carr-Gomm in his office, the man looks out the window, pensively. "Can you imagine the kind of life he must have had?"

"Yes, I think I can—"

"I don't believe so. No one could possibly imagine it. I don't believe any of us can."

This scene came back to me years later when we lived in Southern California and spent Sunday mornings at church helping with a class of mentally disadvantaged people who ranged in age from ten to forty-five years old. There were some with Down's Syndrome, some with varying degrees of autism, and some who seemed tormented by voices they heard or things they saw.

One of the boys was particularly tormented, and from time to time he would scream out and point to what he thought were snakes. He was genuinely terrified, and it took a while to calm him down. Generally you could do that by taking him for a walk and praying for him.

Another boy was obsessed with roller coasters, and that seemed to be all he ever wanted to talk about. He could rattle off all kinds of facts about them, which one was the biggest, the oldest, which one had the most loops. He loved you to gently rub his back, and he especially loved our kids to rub it. They were young at the time and a little afraid of him because sometimes he felt hurt if you didn't give him your whole attention, and sometimes he got angry.

The ones in their late thirties and early forties had maybe the educational level of a first- or second-grader. Because of that, we had to aim our crafts and our music and our lesson for the day at somewhere around that age group.

Some were in wheelchairs and so disfigured that they couldn't talk or participate in anything. There wasn't much you could do except talk kindly to them and stroke their arm or something like that.

One of the boys was about thirteen and in one of those wheelchairs. He could participate in some things, and we tried to involve him as much as possible. He couldn't talk clearly, couldn't hold anything very well in his hand, and was a little bent over. At times I thought I read frustration on his face, but it was hard to tell, and there was a roomful of people that demanded our attention.

One day when I was talking to him, he strained to say something, almost as if he were confiding in me. I strained to listen. "I . . . I . . . mmmm . . . noooot . . . like . . . dem." He said it again, and this time I understood.

"I am not like them" is what he said.

I should have known that. I was his teacher, and I should have known that. I had met his parents only in passing, and it seemed we always had our hands so full that there wasn't an opportunity to ask them about their son. Cerebral palsy is what he had. There was nothing at all wrong with him mentally. His body had imprisoned him, but his mind was as sharp as any thirteen-year-old, maybe sharper, who knows?

I felt terrible when I realized that. Who could imagine what kind of life he has had? How many conversations had he overheard of people talking about him as if he didn't understand a word, when in fact he understood every word? How humiliating for a teenager to listen to music that's aimed at first-graders, to be included in sometimes preschool crafts, to listen to flannel board presentations.

There's no closure to this story. It makes me sad every time I think of it. The awkwardness of how to befriend this boy ended when we left the class and turned the responsibility over to someone else. For him, though, the awkwardness never ends. Or the humiliation. Hearing everything, yet never being heard. Understanding everything, yet never being understood. Always on the outside of everything, except a class like ours.

The other part of *The Elephant Man* that particularly touched me came at the ending. Leading up to the ending is a scene with Merrick in his room, looking up at the steeple of a gothic cathedral. Beneath the window on his desk is a replica of the cathedral that he has been working on for some time. He looks at a sketch on his wall of a child kneeling beside his bed, praying. Then at another picture where the same boy is now asleep in his bed.

Merrick had always wished he could sleep like that, like normal people, but because of the difficulties he had with breathing, he couldn't. He had learned from Treves, who had become his good friend, that he was incurable. The best the hospital could do was to care for him.

By now Merrick has become somewhat of a celebrity in London. Out of that notoriety comes a friendship with a famous actress named Mrs. Kendal (Anne Bancroft) who invites him to be her guest at the theater. Merrick is mesmerized by the stage play. When it ends, Kendal steps onstage and introduces Merrick to the audience of well-bred Londoners. They give him a standing ovation. When Treves escorts him back to his room, you can tell by Merrick's childlike excitement that this night was the high point of his life.

After he says goodbye to his friend, Merrick pauses in front of the handcrafted cathedral. He adds one final touch by signing his name. And it is finished. As Samuel Barber's "Adagio for Strings" begins to play, you have a feeling that Merrick is somehow finished too. That his life is now full and complete.

The camera pans slowly across the cathedral he has made, first horizontally, then vertically, almost as if it were making the sign of a cross. On its vertical descent, the camera moves down the uppermost steeple and rests on a lower one, framing the cross that stands on top of it.

Merrick touches his head in response to what seems a sudden throb of pain. He looks at the picture on the wall of the child sleeping. Then slowly, methodically, he takes the pillows off his bed, one by one. He pulls down the covers. Smoothes the sheet. Crawls into bed. He sits there a moment, then lies down. As "Adagio for Strings" plays on, the camera frames him, giving us a few last moments with this beautiful human being that has been imprisoned in that body for the past twenty-seven years. Slowly the camera moves from him to a picture of Mrs. Kendal, then onto a picture of his mother, onto the cathedral, then upward into the sky.

The way the filmmaker shot the final scene underscores the sanctity of this man's life. The cathedral. The cross. The picture of the child sleeping. The music.

Precious to the Lord is the death of His godly ones, the psalmist says, and as you watch the final moments before John Merrick's death, you sense not only the sacredness of his life but the preciousness of his death in the eyes of God.

It is a holy moment.

That, I think, is why no one left the theater. They sensed something sacred was being shown them. In a sermon titled "The Weight of Glory," C.S. Lewis said that "next to the Blessed Sacrament, your neighbor is the holiest thing presented to your senses."

Treves seemed to have felt that way, at least in regard to this neighbor. "The spirit of Merrick," he wrote in his memoirs, "if it could be seen in the form of the living, it would assume the figure of an upstanding heroic man, smooth-browed and clean of limb, and with eyes that flashed undaunted courage."

The audience that I was a part of seemed to have felt that way too. It were as if a great person had died, and we were the privileged few to be at his bedside when he did. We all left the theater quietly, reverently, a little more human than we were when we came.

Reflections on
The Dead Poets Society

The battle cry of the summer of '89 was "Carpe diem," *the Latin phrase for* "Seize the day." *It came from* Dead Poets Society, *an unlikely summer hit movie about a group of prep school boys. Some audience members reported making new life decisions as a result of seeing the film. Teachers were inspired. Everyone fondly remembered the teachers of their past. Virtually no one walked out of the theater unmoved or unaffected.* [1]

From Script to Screen *by Linda Seger and Edward Jay Whetmore*

In an interview discussing *The Dead Poets Society*, producer Steven Haft said, "The movie affected people in powerful ways. Every time I went to a party and someone introduced me as the producer of *Dead Poets Society*, there would be another story of a person who saw it and left a job, or made some serious life change.

"I can remember the moment when the film's impact really crystallized for me. My wife and I were in New York, walking down the street with Robin [Williams] and his wife, Marsha. This middle-aged man came up to Robin and simply said, 'Thank you,' for *Dead Poets*. Robin bowed to him slightly and turned to me and smiled. He told me there was a definite difference in how people approached him about this film versus his other work.

Usually people say, 'Hey, great film,' and so on. And that's fine. But with this picture it was always 'Thank you.'" 2

Film invites dialogue. That, I think, is why this movie was particularly life-changing for a lot of people. It engaged them in a dialogue about their life.

There were pauses the director structured into the film that gave the audience an opportunity to enter into that conversation. I especially remember the one classroom scene where Professor Keating talks to his students about passion, huddling them all around him. "The powerful play goes on," he tells them, "and each of us can contribute a verse."

Keating pauses long enough to let that thought sink in, then repeats it. "The powerful play goes on, and each of us can contribute a verse."

Another pause, then a question.

"What will *your* verse be?"

Keating looks right at Ethan Hawke's character when he asks it. That is where the director lets the camera rest for maybe an extra beat longer than might be expected. In that extra beat, you are not wondering what Ethan Hawke's verse will be, you're wondering what yours will be.

And you're not sure.

Which would be okay, except you're not a kid in prep school. You're thirtysomething or fortysomething and should have a verse by now. But you don't, and that's a little unsettling.

At some point in that powerful play, our character steps onstage. Between our cue to "Enter" and our cue to "Exit," we have a part in the unfolding drama of redemption. But none of us really knows how big a part.

If I were to audition for a part in a story, say, *To Kill a Mockingbird*, I would want to play Atticus Finch, the lawyer everyone respects, who has a great part to play and great lines to deliver. God, of course, may have different casting plans. Maybe He's looking for someone to play Boo Radley, a misunderstood man with the mind of a child. He has only a few short scenes. We see him in his house, in the shadows, hiding behind the door in Jem's room, and finally sitting with Scout on a porch swing at her house. Boo has no lines to speak. His purpose in the story, as determined by the author, is to save Scout and Jem from the vengeance of Bob Ewell, which in the end he does. Who would have thought Boo would have ever amounted to anything, least of all a hero?

But then, who would have thought Rahab would have amounted to anything either? When Moses sent two men to spy out Jericho, they hid in the house of Rahab the harlot. When the king of Jericho learned this, he ordered her to hand over the men. At great risk to her own life, she told him the men had already left. As the soldiers roamed the city in search, she lowered a rope from her window, allowing Joshua and Caleb to escape. She had only one scene and only a few lines in that scene. Her entire story amounted to a little over a page.

And how about the thief on the cross? He had only one verse: "Remember me when You come in Your kingdom" (Luke 23:42). A seemingly insignificant verse, heard by only a small audience. And yet, how many prisoners awaiting execution have come to Christ because of that one verse? How many people on their deathbeds have looked to that thief, thinking that if he had a chance at getting into heaven, maybe there is hope for them? And maybe this Jesus would accept them on the basis of such a simple expression of faith, who knows?

The life of the thief on the cross was pulp fiction. Rahab's life was a Harlequin romance. Paul's life, before the Damascus Road, was Pulitzer Prize–winning autobiography. Yet none of those were God's story. If you were able to ask the thief, I'm sure he would say he'd rather have that one sentence in God's story than a thousand pages in his own.

It is a humbling realization that sometimes a fragment of our life is all that is useful to God in the story He is telling. When I think about my life, I think of it in terms of a miniseries with a to-die-for role that Richard Chamberlain is champing at the bit to play. I think those things until I see my life from God's perspective, as did Dietrich Bonhoeffer, a Lutheran minister who openly opposed Hitler during World War II.

While Bonhoeffer was imprisoned in a German concentration camp, he reflected on his life, wondering what the deeper meaning of it might be. It seemed to him so confusing. The fragments of his life seemed disconnected, like sentences in search of a story. A few months before his execution, he came to this conclusion. "It all depends on whether or not the fragment of our life reveals the plan and material of the whole. There are fragments which are only good to be thrown away, and others which are important for centuries to come, because their fulfillment can only be a divine work. They are fragments of necessity. If our life, however remotely, reflects such a fragment . . . we shall not have to bewail our fragmentary life, but, on the contrary, to rejoice in it." [3]

When we look at our life from that perspective, even the most fragmentary parts may have eternal significance. What *The Dead Poets Society* does particularly well is to challenge us to look at life from a little different perspective than what we are used to, as in the scene where Professor Keating has his students stand on his desk to look at the classroom through new eyes. In the process of looking at life from a different perspective, it causes us to look at our own lives from a different perspective too. The movie does this primarily through the main character, Professor Keating.

Keating, himself a graduate of the boarding school where he now teaches, is new to the faculty. It is his romantic view of life that sets up the conflict between himself and his more traditional colleagues, eventually leading to his dismissal. He is, in every sense of the word, a nontraditionalist. You know that the very first day of class. He enters the room from his office in the front of the class, walks past a row of students, whistling while he walks, and leaves the classroom. He steps back in and calls to them, "Well, come on."

The boys hesitate to follow, but one by one they do. As they spill into the hallway, Keating is standing in front of a trophy case. Once he has their attention, he asks Mr. Pitt to read a page from the textbook on poetry.

Gather ye rosebuds while you may,
Old time is still a-flying.
And this same flower that smiles today,
Tomorrow will be dying.

"The Latin term for that sentiment is *carpe diem*," he tells them.

He asks for a translation, and one of the students says, "*Carpe diem,* seize the day."

"Why does the writer use these words, 'Gather ye rosebuds while you may'? Because we are food for worms, lads. Believe it or not, each and every one in this room will one day stop breathing, turn cold, and die."

As Keating tells them this, the camera becomes their eyes as they study the faces on an old, faded photograph of a bygone basketball team. "Look at the pictures in the trophy case. Same haircuts. Same raging hormones. They believe they are destined for great things, just like you. Invincible, just like you. Eyes full of hope, just like you."

Their eyes drift to a team picture of football players.

"These boys are now fertilizing daffodils. If you listen real close, you can hear them whispering their legacy to you." As the students lean in, Keating whispers the haunting words, "'*Car-pe . . . car-pe . . . carpe diem*. Make your lives extraordinary.'"

It is the most memorable moment in the film. One generation face-to-face with another. Looking through the glass at one another. Studying one another. There is great drama in this moment, and when Keating whispers their legacy, the effect is powerful.

It is a defining moment for some of those who are transfixed by the photographs in that trophy case. And for some of those in the audience too.

I love that moment. I love the quiet drama that is created by their unspoken dialogue with those photographs. I also love the imperatives, "seize the day" and "make your life extraordinary."

Here is what I struggle with in that scene. I don't know about you, but the thought of my life being fertilizer for daffodils doesn't seem the most compelling argument for making my life extraordinary.

The argument is a fashionable form of hedonism, wearing a coat and tie instead of a toga. Seizing the day because we're all going to end up as food for worms is not exactly the same as "eat, drink, and be merry, for tomorrow we die." But it's not a whole lot different either.

There are other philosophical options for seizing the day that are, in my opinion, better than the one the movie gives us. Jesus promised to give us not only life but life in its fullness, its richness, its abundance. That should be our reason for seizing the day. The day is a gift, given us from the generous hand of God. And we are to receive it as the incalculable treasure it is, take hold of it, and enjoy it to the fullest.

Just as we have gifts to receive from the day, we also have gifts to give. Gifts of love. Of understanding. And compassion. Of kindness. And forgiveness. Of wonder. And gratitude. This, I think, is how we make our lives extraordinary. By the gifts we give and joyful generosity with which we give them.

In spite of my philosophical differences with the scene at the trophy case, I still love it. To be fair, there's a lot of truth in it. The truth is, our life on this earth is ephemeral (James 4:14) and we will be food for worms (Psalm 90:3). For a while, anyway, but not forever (1 Corinthians 15).

That moment in the movie changed the way I look at a number of things. I take more time when I look at photographs, for one thing, especially old, faded ones. I look into the eyes of those flat, black-and-white faces and wonder what dreams once lay behind them, what hopes, what fears, what joys, what sorrows. I study the lines on their faces and wonder what all they have weathered before that one day when they stopped breathing, turned cold, and died.

I look at the photographs, and I listen to them because I think they might have something to say, and maybe some of what they have to say is meant for me. I'm not sure I ever listened to what a photograph had to say until I saw that scene with the trophy case.

A trophy case was one of the things I went to see on one of my trips back home to Fort Worth. I stopped at the high school I attended. It was a large school when I went there, some 2,400 students. As I walked the floors, I was amazed how much of the past came back to me through things as slight as the sound of an oscillating fan or the smell of chalk dust or the sheen of polished linoleum.

I'm not sure why I go back or what I'm looking for when I do, but often when I go home, I'll touch something of the past while I'm there. It might be the old neighborhood one trip. The elementary school another trip. The church where I went to Boy Scout meetings on Monday nights. The route I took when I sometimes walked home from school. Some place where we used to shop.

This time, though, it was the high school.

The high school was three stories of weathered red brick with white wood trim, a football field, baseball field, and a small gym. Seeing those things reminded me of the wealth of gifted athletes the school had. One of the students won an Olympic bronze medal in swimming. The golf and tennis teams were among the best in the state of Texas. The baseball team lost 1-0 in the state finals. And the football team went to regionals. Basketball—my sport—was the only one that didn't win district the year I graduated.

That year alone the school had accumulated enough honors to fill a trophy case. I thought I'd stop to study the case the way Keating's students had studied theirs. I had never done that before. Even when I had gone to school there, I never stopped to look. I hoped not only to look at them but to listen to what they might have to say.

I looked, but they weren't there. The trophies from that year were all gone. Only a generation has passed, and the memories of that generation have already been boxed away. Who knows where they might be? They may be lost, possibly forever. It was then that the truth of the scene from *The Dead Poets Society* seemed so blindingly true it hurt to look at it.

What made that day at my high school so unforgettable was a funeral I was going to. It was the funeral of a man who had been a star athlete for the school. He played three sports and excelled in all of them. All-district quarterback and captain of the football team. Basketball honors, baseball. Outstanding student. President of the student body. He was the All-American boy and was at least partly responsible for several of those trophies.

Now, not only were the trophies gone, he was gone.

He was two years older than me, but I knew him because for a while we had been part-time janitors together at the school. Years later he attended the small church that I pastored. He died in his sleep of a heart attack. News of his death came as a shock because he was always in such great shape.

What made that weekend even more unusual was that I had seen him, coincidentally, on an infomercial the day before I traveled to Fort Worth. He had been dead only a day, and yet there he was, talking on TV. It was surreal. The infomercial was promoting ostrich and emu ranching, of all things, and as I was driving through West Texas, I saw a dozen of those ranches. It was an odd sight because I was used to seeing cattle and horses whenever I drove through that part of the state, so each time I passed a herd of those gawky-looking birds, I did a double-take.

News of his death, the infomercial, the ostrich ranches, his funeral, and that day at my high school all came together during a period of about four days. It was all too coincidental to be coincidental, if that at all makes sense.

It was impossible not to think about those things. And thinking about them, it was impossible not to think that maybe God was trying to get my attention, to tell me something.

I'm not sure exactly what He was trying to say, but if I heard right, it sounded something like *carpe diem*. Because none of us knows how many days have been allotted for us or how many opportunities we will have to seize them.

I never had a professor like Mr. Keating. And I never attended a school like the one in *The Dead Poets Society*. Seminary came pretty close, though. Like the prep school, ours required us to wear a coat and tie. And like the prep school, the curriculum was very structured, the classes very organized, the teachers very formal. We didn't eat in a great hall like the prep school did, but every day we did go to chapel in a great cavernous building where we had assigned seats and people watching over them whose job it was to make note of any empty ones and report them to somebody who thought it egregious enough of an infraction to be worth reporting.

Like the prep school, seminary had its blind spots.

But it also had its bright spots.

For me, those were a few friends and a few professors.

One of those professors was the polar opposite of Professor Keating, and the first truly brilliant person I had ever met. He was so brilliant that when he finished his Ph.D. at Harvard, they asked him to stay and teach there. He declined, returning to teach at the seminary instead, and the seminary was richer because of it. He was held in the highest esteem by the faculty and in absolute awe by the student body.

He would begin class with a prayer, then open the Hebrew text, picking up where our last class with him had left off. He had lived so much in the text that he was completely at home there. In the classroom he was like a farmer in regard to the rich soil of the Old Testament, and we students were the plow he used to till it. Not an easy task, given how dull the blades can be on any given morning.

He worked the ground methodically. Sometimes, especially in his Isaiah class, he would go down a row, one student after the other. If you didn't know the answer to his question, he passed the question to the next student, then to the next student, until one of the students answered correctly. The line of questioning went something like this.

"Isaiah 40, verse 1. Mr. [and he called someone's last name], read the Hebrew please." As the student read, you could almost see the beads of sweat forming on his forehead. And when he was done, you could almost hear his sigh of relief. Between the sweat and the sighs, the professor would stop the student if he stumbled over a word or put the accent on the wrong syllable. He might correct him or ask one of the other students for the correct answer.

"Mr. Johnson [or whoever it was in the next desk], translate." Again, the professor would quiz the student on the tense of the verb if he got it wrong, or add a little color to a word if the student's rendering seemed a little pale. Again, the beads of sweat, followed by the sigh of relief.

"Articulate the lexical problem, Mr.—"

"What is the grammatical anomaly—"

"Articulate the theological tension—"

More sweat, more sighs.

When I was taking a course of his on the Psalms, he said something that caused a Copernican shift in my thinking. Here are the words that lead to the shift.

"Next we come to the great theological word *yirah*," he said, "the fear of the Lord. What is 'the fear of the Lord'?" He proceeded to answer his own question, and we all breathed a sigh of relief. He started with the Old Testament, going then to the New, and ending up in the present with its application for those of us students who would soon be deciding on such things as majors and ministries.

I have forgotten many of the things I learned in that professor's classes. But I haven't forgotten that particular day in class or what he said. He said simply: "What we produce will fail. But what happens to us in the producing of it is eternal."

As students, it seemed to us that those decisions about our future were of paramount importance. Our professor gave us a different way of looking at them. What he was trying to show us was this. The sermons or books or churches we might one day produce weren't nearly as important as what would happen to us in the producing of them. That is what's eternal. And it's the eternity of our lives, not the futility of them, that should motivate us to seize the day and live extraordinary lives.

That is a little different message than the one in *The Dead Poets Society*.

When we leave this world, the trophies get left behind. It doesn't make any difference whether the trophies are for athletic, academic, or artistic achievement, or some other kind of achievement.

The only things that go with us are the things produced *in* us.

The Dead Poets Society made me think about pictures in trophy cases in ways I had never done before. In doing so, it made me think about my own life in ways I had never done before.

For that, I am truly grateful.

I can't say that about all of the dialogue. In spite of how different Professor Keating was from my Hebrew professor, it is my professor's words, not Keating's, that have motivated me to want to seize the day and make my life extraordinary.

For that, I am *eternally* grateful.

Reflections on *Amistad*

There is a moment in every great story in which the presence of grace can be felt as it waits to be accepted or rejected, even though the reader may not recognize this moment. [1]

FLANNERY O'CONNOR

Mystery and Manners

A lawyer once asked Jesus what was the greatest of all commandments. Jesus said that the first and foremost commandment is: "'You shall love the Lord your God with all your heart, and with all your soul, and with all your mind.' And a second is like it, 'You shall love your neighbor as yourself.' On these two commandments depend the whole Law and the Prophets."

What movies do best, I think, is to help us understand our neighbor, which is the first step to loving our neighbor. If we can see the characters on the screen, *really* see them, if we can laugh with them, cry with them, understand them, and to some degree love them, perhaps we can take something of what we've experienced in the theater into the world and learn to see people, to understand them, and to love them.

I can better understand and therefore better love my Jewish neighbor if I know the stories of Egypt and Masada and Auschwitz. I can better love my

Native American brother if I know the stories of Sand Creek and Washita and Wounded Knee. And I can better love my African-American brother if I know the stories of Africa and the slave trade and the *Amistad*.

Like *Saving Private Ryan* and *Schindler's List, Amistad* has violent scenes that are difficult to watch. Is the violence necessary? I don't see how the story could be told without it. If the filmmaker shielded our eyes from the violence, he would be shielding us from the truth. And though we pay a price if we look at the violence, we pay a price if we don't. We may protect our hearts by not exposing them to such images, but in doing so, we may prevent our hearts from growing.

The presence of grace waits within every great story, as Flannery O'Conner said. When that story is truthfully told, it releases the power of grace, and that is how a moment in a story changes us.

But how much we should allow ourselves to see and to hear in order to be changed is an issue we all wrestle with. There are basic standards we all have, not just because we're Christians but because we're human beings. Although, I've found, it's usually not the black-and-white things we struggle with. It's the gray and the various shades of gray. In such cases I think we should defer to Paul's advice in Romans 14. Though we may have different convictions about such things (vv. 1-5a), and though those convictions are private (v. 4), we should be certain about the convictions we have (v. 5b).

All that being said, I would like to say this, which is often left unsaid.

Our faith is based on a public execution that was filled with foul language, full-frontal nudity, and unbearable violence.

I would never want my children to go there and be exposed to such things.

But *I* would want to go there. I would want to stand with John and Mary and the other women who stood there, watching, weeping, praying for a quick and merciful end to it all.

I would want Jesus, when He had the strength to open His eyes, to see that He was surrounded by the faces of those who loved Him. And I would want one of those faces to be mine. I would want to be there so I could look into His eyes, and so He could look into mine. I would want to be there to tell Him how much I loved Him, and hope that, at some point, He would have the strength to tell me. I would want to hear what He had to say to God who had forsaken Him, to the thieves who had cursed Him, and to the soldiers who had crucified Him. I would want to be there so I would never forget what happened there. I would want to see how He suffered and how He died, because it was for *me* that He suffered and for *me* that He died.

What we see whenever we see a movie about Jesus are scenes that look more like an Easter pageant than a Roman crucifixion. I'm not sure how many people come away from a pageant changed. But from that crucifixion scene, I know that at least a thief came away changed . . . and a centurion . . . and a disciple who went on to write more about God's love than all the other disciples combined.

There are several scenes in *Amistad* that have within them the power to change a person's life, or at least some part of it. Before I describe one of those scenes, though, let me set it in context.

In February 1839, slave traders from Portugal abducted a group of Africans from Sierra Leone with the intent of shipping them to Havana, a thriving center of slave trade. Fifty-three Africans were purchased by two Spanish planters, then shipped by the Cuban vessel *Amistad* to be delivered to a plantation in the Caribbean. On July 1, the Africans killed the captain and the cook, seized control of the ship, and ordered the planters to sail them back to Africa. But on August 24, the *Amistad* was seized by a U.S. vessel off the coast of New York.

The case went to the Supreme Court in *United States v. The Amistad,* March 9, 1841, which ruled that the Africans onboard the *Amistad* were free individuals, that they had been kidnapped and transported illegally and had never been slaves. The court ordered their immediate release, and early in 1842, they were returned to their homeland.

The Africans had been imprisoned on charges of murder. Though the murder charges were later dismissed, they continued to be held captive on the basis of being property that could be legally claimed under certain salvage rights. The fate of this human property was to be determined by trial.

At that trial, Cinque, the one who led the revolt on the ship, stands up, and in an emotionally charged moment, calls out to the court: "Give us free! . . . Give us free!"

But they are not given their freedom. They are returned to their prison where they must await a verdict. In the dark recesses of the prison, one of the men named Jamba is looking through a Bible that had been given him by one of the Christian abolitionists. The scene in the prison is intercut with a scene in the church where the judge goes to pray and seek God's guidance about the case.

Cinque calls to Jamba from across the room: "You don't have to pretend to be interested in that. Nobody's watching but me."

Jamba says: "I'm not pretending. I'm beginning to understand it."

Being African, he can't read the English Bible. All he can do is look at the

illustrations. From those pictures he pieces together the story. The first picture is one where several Jews that have been thrown to the lions. Cinque has
come to his side now and is looking at the pictures with him.

Jamba explains: "Their lives have suffered more that ours. . . . Their lives
were full of suffering."

He turns to the next picture, which is one where the baby Jesus is lying
in the manager, surrounded by Mary, Joseph, and the shepherds.

"Then *he* was born and everything changed."

"Who is he?" asks Cinque.

Jamba turns the page to a picture of Jesus riding on a donkey to
Jerusalem, a halo of light circling his head.

"I don't know, but everywhere he goes, he is followed by the sun."

He turns to the next picture. Jesus is touching people who appear to be
sick or afflicted in some way.

"Here he is healing people with his hands."

Jamba turns to the next page, where Jesus is standing between the
woman caught in adultery and the crowd that is waiting to stone her.

"Protecting them . . ."

He turns to the next picture, and it is one where Jesus is blessing the
children.

"Being given children . . ."

He turns the Bible sideways as there is a long picture this time, one of
Jesus walking on the water.

"What's this?" asks Cinque.

"He could also walk across the sea. But then something happened. He
was captured. Accused of some crime."

He points to a picture that shows Jesus before Pilate and the people.

"Here he is with his hands tied."

Cinque shakes his head. "He must have done something."

"Why? What did he do? Whatever it was, it was serious enough to kill him for it. Do you want to see how they killed him?"

He turns to the next picture where Jesus is hanging on a cross between two thieves.

"This is just a story, Jamba."

"But look. That's not the end of it."

They both peer into a picture of Jesus' limp body as it is being taken off the cross.

"His people took his body down from this . . . thing . . . this. . . ." Jamba makes the sign of a cross to explain. "They took him into a cave. They wrapped him in a cloth like we do."

He turns to the next picture, which shows Jesus on the Emmaus road with two disciples. Cinque watches quietly as Jamba explains.

"They thought he was dead, but he appeared before his people again . . . and spoke to them. Then, finally, he rose into the sky."

The next picture is of the Ascension.

"This is where the soul goes when you die here," Jamba explains.

He turns the page, and the picture shows Jesus in heaven.

"This is where we're going when they kill us. It doesn't look so bad."

He turns to the next picture, which displays three empty crosses. And they linger over it a moment. The series of pictures form a striking illustration of Hebrews 12:3, "For consider Him who has endured such hostility by sinners against Himself, so that you may not grow weary and lose heart."

Which is what Jamba and Cinque are doing, considering Him, and gaining strength in doing so.

The scene abruptly changes to the prisoners being shackled together in chains and led out into the street. All shuffle down the street, several of them with their heads down. Cinque calls to one of them.

"Hold your head up."

They pass a group of nuns with crosses in outstretched hands. Cinque looks to the buildings and sees behind them three bare masts of the ship that took them from their homeland, reminding him of the three empty crosses that Jamba had showed him.

The two scenes had a powerful effect on me. I don't think I've ever seen the story of Christ told on film in such a clear, concise, and compelling way. The beauty of it was breathtaking. The black-and-white illustrations by Gustave Doré had a solemnity to them that fit the fate of the prisoners.

As Jamba and Cinque talked about the pictures, they spoke in their own language. English subtitles translated the conversation, and the fact that you read the words in silence somehow gave the words greater resonance.

As Flannery O'Connor said, "There is a moment in every great story in which the presence of grace can be felt as it waits to be accepted or rejected, even though the reader may not recognize this moment."

Amistad was one of those great stories. This was one of the great moments in that story. I felt the presence of grace. And I think it was one of those rare occasions when everyone who saw it felt it too.

Reflections on
Schindler's List

Remembrance is the seed of redemption.

ISRAEL BA'AL SHEM TOV

The founder of Hasidism

I first heard the stories from my father. Whenever we walked together, he told me stories, and the ones I found especially riveting were his war stories. One evening, though, he told me a different story about the war.

He was in the 36th Infantry Division of the Army, and near the end of the war his battery helped liberate a concentration camp. I forget its name, and he has been dead now for fourteen years, so that part of the story is gone. The part that remains is what he saw when he entered the camp. The prisoners were little more than skeletons covered with skin. He told me of the atrocities the Nazis inflicted upon the Jews, how they starved them, worked them to death, gassed them, and performed experiments on them. He told me how they made lampshades from their skin and soap from their fat.

It all seemed too horrible to be true, but later I saw some of the film footage on television. It *was* true. Since then, everything he told me that night has been validated by the books I have read and the films I have seen.

In an attempt to help the starving prisoners at that concentration camp, the American soldiers gave them their C-rations. Within minutes their stomachs swelled. Several died. Because their bodies had not been used to solid food, they started bloating the minute the rations hit their stomachs. In an attempt to save as many as they could, the soldiers punctured their stomachs with their bayonets so the gas could escape. It was much easier to treat the wound than it was to keep the bloat from killing them.

The order was promptly issued not to give the prisoners any more solid food. Instead they gave them water. Later, clear broth. Later still, soup.

My dad saw 287 straight days of combat. Part of that time he was in Italy as a member of the artillery battery at the battle of Cassino. He came home with a Bronze Star and a Purple Heart, which he kept in one of his drawers. Many times I would get them out when no one was home and reverently rub my fingers over them. I had always been proud of my father for fighting in that war, but I was never more proud than the night he told me about his part in helping to liberate that camp.

The loss of life from the concentration camps was staggering. By the war's end, two out of three European Jews were dead. Nine out of ten in Poland, Lithuania, Latvia, Czechoslovakia. Relatively few survivors remain. Each year there are fewer still. In twenty-five years, all of them will be gone. What we will be left with then are only the stories they have left behind.

The stories may come in some form of art, like *Schindler's List,* or literature, like Elie Wiesel's *Night,* or in some form of recorded testimony, like Claude Lanzmann's documentary *Shoah.* If we don't read the literature that has been written about the Holocaust, if we don't see the art, if we don't hear the testimonies, the Holocaust will fade from memory.

The dedication page of the book *The World Must Know: A History of the Holocaust as Told in the Holocaust Memorial Museum* by Michael Berenbaum reads: "In memory of those who were consumed by the Holocaust. May their memory serve as a blessing—and a warning." [1] The warning is that if the stories are not remembered, this darkest of chapters in human history could very well be repeated.

Claude Lanzmann was a filmmaker who dedicated eleven years of his life to making sure the stories were remembered. The finished product is a documentary titled *Shoah,* the Hebrew word for "annihilation." It is a nine-and-a-half-hour collection of interviews of Jews who survived the Holocaust, Poles who lived around the camps, and former Nazis and SS officers. I saw it one week while I was in Los Angeles, and I was surprised that there was no archival footage. The film consisted solely of present-day interviews.

What Lanzmann did with this film was to usher person after person to the witness stand, letting the audience be the jury of those who perpetrated such horrible crimes against humanity. He is the one asking the questions, calling witness after witness after witness, the same way a trial lawyer slowly builds his case. Like any courtroom trial, the questions at first seem inconsequential:

> "Describe the gas vans."
> "Who were the drivers?"
> "Were there many of these drivers?"
> "Were there two, three, five, ten?"
> "Did the driver sit in the cab or the van?"
> "Did he race the motor?"

"Could you hear the sound of the motor?"

"Was it a loud noise?"

The questions seem irrelevant, and we wonder, *Where is all this leading?*

It is leading to the scenes of the crimes—Auschwitz, Treblinka, Buchenwald, Sobibor, Belzec, Chelmno—to establish beyond question the guilt of the criminals.

Steven Spielberg launched a somewhat similar project after making *Schindler's List*, in which he invited Holocaust survivors to tell their stories on film, uncut and unedited, so that the stories could be archived for future generations.

Again the words of Michael Berenbaum: "Only remembrance could salvage some meaning from the ashes of Auschwitz. The dead had died merely for the accident of their Jewish ancestry. Their deaths could serve as a warning, but only if the story was told from generation to generation." [2]

From one generation to the next, my father told me the story, and I, in turn, told it to my children. One of the ways my wife and I told them was through the book *Number the Stars* by Lois Lowry, the all-but-forgotten story of the heroic efforts of the Danish people to evacuate seven thousand Jews to safety in Sweden. Another way was through a Symphony of Remembrance we took them to, which displayed some of the prison garb, some of the art, and some of the personal belongings of those who perished in the camps. Another way was through the movie *Schindler's List*. A difficult call for a parent, but that is the call we made, and I believe that for our family it was a good call.

It is a hard movie to watch. It should be hard. The subject demands it to be hard. It also demands we look and not turn away. Aleksandr Solzhenitsyn explains why: "The sole substitute for an experience which we have not ourselves lived through is art and literature. Both are endowed with the miraculous power to communicate—despite differences in language, custom, and social structure—the experience of the entire nation to another nation which has not undergone such a difficult decades-long collective experience. In a fortunate instance, this could save an entire nation from a redundant, or erroneous, or even destructive course, thereby shortening the tortuous paths of human history." [3]

Someone once said that those who forget history are condemned to repeat it. Conversely, those who remember history are constrained to redeem it. For remembrance delivers a nation from repeating the sins of previous nations.

Schindler's List is a work of remembrance. It was adapted from Thomas Keneally's book of the same name. Released in 1993, the film won seven Academy Awards, including best picture, best director, and best adapted screenplay. The story is based on the life of Oskar Schindler, a German entrepreneur whose labor force was composed entirely of Jews whom he rescued from being sent to the camps by conscripting them as workers in his factory. During the course of the war, he becomes more allied with his workers than with his country, and through them is changed from a self-seeking man to a self-sacrificing one. He was a womanizer, a drunk, and a spendthrift. He also saved more European Jews than anyone else except for Raoul Wallenberg.

There were so many moving scenes in the film, but the one that moved me the most was Schindler's final scene. When the unconditional surrender of Germany to the Allied Forces is announced, Schindler gathers his workers along with the German soldiers who were stationed there. Addressing them, he stands resolutely and speaks courageously. In the next scene we see a different Oskar Schindler.

It is past midnight, and a car is waiting to take Schindler (Liam Neeson) and his wife away. All his workers surround them. The have all signed a letter explaining things if he were captured. Earlier, several of them volunteered to have the gold fillings in their teeth extracted to make a ring.

Giving the ring to Schindler, Itzhak Stern (Ben Kingsley) translates the Hebrew inscription, a quote from the Talmud: "It says, 'Whoever saves one life, saves the world entire.'"

Schindler is overwhelmed. He says to Stern, "I could've got more out . . . I could've got more . . . if I'd just . . . I don't know, if I'd just . . . I could've got more. . . ."

"Oskar, there are eleven hundred people who are alive because of you. Look at them."

But he can't because he is overcome by the reality of so many opportunities that he has squandered. "If I'd made more money . . . I threw away so much money, you have no idea. If I'd just . . ."

"There will be generations because of what you did," Stern says compassionately.

"I didn't do enough."

"You did so much."

Schindler weeps. "This car. Goeth would've bought this car. Why did I keep the car? Ten people, right there, ten more I could've got." He looks around him, then down at his lapel. "This pin. . . . " He pulls the swastika from his lapel and holds it out to Stern. "Two people. This is gold. Two more people. He would've given me two for it. At least one. He would've given me one. One more. One more person. A person, Stern. For this. One more. I could've gotten one more person and I didn't."

Schindler continues to weep. "They killed so many people. . . . " He breaks down, sobbing on his knees, and Stern embraces him. "They killed so many people. . . ."

A woman comes and kneels beside him. Then another. And another. Schindler finally gets up and changes clothes from his lavish suit to a plain prison uniform. He and his wife get into the car, and the driver takes them away. As he looks at his workers, his face is reflected in the glass. It is powerful scene. Good has triumphed over evil. Life has defeated death. Humanity has won out over inhumanity. And all of this is captured, not in a celebratory moment, but in a solemn one. It is a humble scene, full of human kindness, which is made visible in Stern's tender response to Schindler's remorse.

As the scene was playing, I couldn't help thinking that this is what it may be like for many of us at the Judgment Seat of Christ, before whom we will appear to give an account of our lives. I think there will be great remorse, great shame, great sadness for all who, like me, have squandered so many opportunities. For those like me who realized so late what life was all about.

It wasn't about making money.

It was about saving lives.

I see myself standing before Christ, weeping, mumbling to myself the way Schindler did to Stern. "I wasted so much time. I could have done more if I hadn't've spent my life so foolishly. One program. I could have cut out one weekly television program, and I would have had so many hours for so many people."

And as I am saying this, I see Jesus, standing before me, not as a harsh judge but as Itzhak Stern. Full of understanding and compassion. Extending mercy by revealing to me what all I had done for Him, not what all I hadn't.

But the sadness of so much of the life I had squandered overwhelms me. "I could've helped more . . . I could've saved more . . . if I'd just . . . I don't know, if I'd just . . . I could've got more. . . ."

"Ken, there are so many who are alive because of you. Look at them."

He will show them to me, but my eyes are too full of tears to see them. "If I just hadn't wasted so much time . . . I threw away so much time, you have no idea. If I'd just . . ."

"There will be generations because of what you did."

He shows me a world of people who had descended from that one person I had helped to save, from that one prayer I had offered to give, from that one act of kindness I had done in His name. And the grace is so great I cannot bear it.

"I didn't do enough."

"You did so much," He says.

And as I fall to my knees, sobbing, He bends down and embraces me.

Maybe my imaginings have been influenced too much by Hollywood endings, I don't know. But while Jesus walked this earth, He was always full of mercy. And that mercy was always offered to those who needed it most but deserved it least. I don't think His going to heaven changed that. And if it is true that mercy triumphs over judgment, then perhaps that scene is less of a Hollywood ending and more of a heavenly one.

Reflections on
The Wizard of Oz

I was sick for the better part of a year with a glittering combination of pneumonia, tonsillitis, and pleurisy, and during the period I was in bed, I lived, as much as I could be said to live anywhere, not in the United States of America but in the Land of Oz. One Oz book after another I read or had read to me until the world where animals can speak, and magic is as common as grass, and no one dies, was so much more real to me than the world of my own room that if I had had the occasion to be homesick then, it would have been for Oz, not home, that I would have been homesick for as in a way I am homesick for it still. [1]

FREDERICK BUECHNER

The Sacred Journey

Originally there were seven pairs of ruby slippers used in the filming of *The Wizard of Oz*. Only five are known to exist today. Each is valued at $1.5 million, making them the most expensive items of Hollywood memorabilia. Another piece of memorabilia, Dorothy's blue-and-white gingham pinafore, sold in 1999 at an auction held by Christie's in London. The winning bid was $324,000. The prices for these pieces of movie history indicate the place the movie occupies in the hearts of the millions who have seen it.

The Wizard of Oz made its film debut in 1939. It made its television debut in 1956. Airing on CBS to 53 percent of the viewing audience, the film spread its magic to forty-five million Americans.

I, an impressionable six-year-old, was one of them.

The film won two Academy Awards, one for best musical score, and one for best song, "Somewhere Over the Rainbow," which had almost been cut from the movie. A special award was given to Judy Garland for an outstanding performance by a teenager.

The Wizard of Oz is one of the few examples, in my opinion, of a movie being better than the book from which it was adapted. Although the book is quite good, the characters in the movie are so much more engaging, especially the Cowardly Lion, who has this wonderfully endearing quality of vacillation.

Cowardly Lion: All right, I'll go in there for Dorothy. Wicked Witch or no Wicked Witch, guards or no guards, I'll tear them apart. I may never come out alive, but I'm going in there. There's only one thing I want you fellows to do.

Tin Woodman and Scarecrow: What's that?

Cowardly Lion: Talk me out of it.

And Judy Garland singing "Somewhere Over the Rainbow," how could a writer ever capture that moment with words? The look in her eyes and the longing in her voice defy translation.

The song is the heart of the movie, and it struck a chord in the heart of an entire generation. A forty-five-year-old psychologist living in New York is representative of the response children had to the song. His mother used to play the piano and sing the words to that song when he was seven or eight years old, playing on the floor with his toys.

"Sometimes," he recalled, "I felt like the music and the images of the words were taking me far, far away from the reality of being a little boy on the floor playing with his toys. There was a yearning quality that somehow deeply touched me. At the same time, I would feel a part of me was already somewhere high above the heavens, 'over the rainbow,' just like the song was saying.

"The sensation that accompanied this awareness was one of complete euphoria—as though I were back in a wonderfully familiar place that I had somehow forgotten in my task of being a growing boy. I felt transported to a timeless place, with sunlight in the sky and a tremendous joy inside me." 2

Something inside us longs for a faraway place where troubles melt like lemon drops and the dreams that we dare to dream really do come true. Besides experiencing the same longing that Dorothy felt, we also have experienced the same exclusion she felt in the opening sequence when Auntie Em says to her: "Now you just help us out today and find yourself a place where you won't get into any trouble."

The forlorn Dorothy Gale has no one to confide in but her dog. She strolls with him from a bale of hay to a piece of farm machinery where they both sit down. "Some place where there isn't any trouble," she says. "Do you suppose there is such a place, Toto? There must be. It's not a place you can get to by a boat or a train. It's far, far away, behind the moon, beyond the rain."

And looking to the sky, she begins to sing.

Somewhere over the rainbow
Way up high,
There's a land that I heard of
Once in a lullaby.

When the sweet, sixteen-year-old Judy Garland sang this song, she sang it for all of us. It's my favorite moment in the film and the moment that set me dreaming for the place she sang about.

In his book on the film, Salman Rushdie wrote: "At the heart of *The Wizard of Oz* is a great tension between two dreams [the dream of home and the dream of leaving home]; but as the music swells and that big clean voice flies into the anguished longings of the song, can anyone doubt which message is the stronger? In its most potent emotional moment, this is unarguably a film about the joys of going away, of leaving the greyness and entering the colour, of making a new life in the 'place where there isn't any trouble.'" [3]

Some place where there isn't any trouble. Do you suppose there could be such a place?

Jesus said there was. It's a real place, a real, truly live place (John 14:2), where there will no longer be any death or mourning or crying or pain (Revelation 21:4). The place is heaven. I believe we have an innate longing for it that is as deeply embedded in us as our genetic code. C.S. Lewis once said: "There have been times when I think we do not desire heaven but more often I find myself wondering whether, in our heart of hearts, we have desired anything else." [4]

Growing up, I learned about heaven pretty much the same way I learned about sex. Nobody talked about sex in the '50s. You couldn't use the word "pregnant" on television, and Lucy and Ricky, along with all the other television parents, wore full-length pajamas and slept in twin beds. So you didn't learn about sex from television. You didn't learn about it from the movies. You didn't learn about it from church. And if you were like most kids, you didn't learn about it from your parents either.

Invariably, you learned it from some older kid in the block or on the bus or from all you're exposed to in that first harrowing year of junior high. In the smoke-filled bathrooms you would find cryptic words etched onto the stalls with hieroglyphics to go with them. Or you heard some of the older boys in P.E. snickering about it. Or you overheard some adults giggling about it until you came into the room, then the voices hushed and the subject changed.

When you finally put all the pieces of the puzzle together, it wasn't a very pretty picture. And when you realized that someday society expected you to do your part to propagate the species, it wasn't something you were exactly looking forward to.

The way I learned about heaven was remarkably similar. I heard words tossed around like "forever," and as a young boy, whenever I thought of forever, I thought of how long Communion Sunday lasted, or how long it was until Christmas, an eternity for any child. So "forever" didn't have a lot of positive associations for me.

The other word I heard in reference to heaven was "singing." In heaven we would be singing praises to God. I grew up in a Lutheran church, and the Lutherans then didn't stick with a few old stalwart standbys as the Baptists did. Lutherans picked their Sunday songs according to the church calendar, so there would be songs for Lent and Palm Sunday, Ascension

Sunday, and so on. It seemed the people in the pews were always either a note in front of the organist or a note behind her. To make matters worse, the organist would try to catch up with them or slow down so they could catch up with her. And for some reason, known only to God, we would sing every verse of those songs that none of us knew or much liked.

Put "singing" and "forever" together, and it can sour a kid on heaven real fast.

Somewhere along the road to growing up, I also heard the phrase, "called home," which, I learned, is what happens when you die. You're called home. Being called home wasn't something a kid looked forward to, not in my neighborhood anyway. All the kids in my neighborhood played after supper, sometimes long past dark. We caught lightning bugs in Mason jars, shagged balls in the street, rode bikes, played hide-and-seek, or just sat on the curb under the streetlight and talked. Being called home put an end to the fun and meant you had to brush your teeth and go to bed.

Heaven as I knew it was Dorothy's Kansas, flat and gray and dull. But if the reports can be believed, it is just the opposite. It is more like the scene in which the tornado plops Dorothy's house down in the Land of Oz. When Dorothy opened the door, the drab monotone of the Kansas countryside was behind her. Before her stretched a world sparkling with color, a world of Emerald Cities and Yellow Brick Roads and enchanted forests. When you think about it, Oz seems less like a fairy tale and more like the land described in the final chapters of Revelation.

As I grew older, I put away most of the childish things of my boyhood. I went to college, then seminary, and by that time I had heard a lot of things about heaven and believed I would someday go there and have an opportunity to see for myself if the rumors were true. Paul, who was the source of some of those rumors, had been granted a glimpse of what awaits us there (2 Corinthians 12:1-4), and he said that eye has not seen or ear heard all that the Lord has prepared for us (1 Corinthians 2:9), that it was a glory so great our sufferings pale in comparison (Romans 8:18).

Like everyone else, I wanted to go to there. But like everyone else, I wanted to experience all that this life had to offer first. I wanted to get married, have sex, have kids, a career. I believed in heaven, but I couldn't honestly say that I longed to go there.

Little by little, though, my longing for heaven was stirred. First by that song in the movie, then by a series of books called The Chronicles of Narnia by C.S. Lewis. By the time we finished reading them, we all wanted to go to Narnia. Here is how the last book in the series ends, when Aslan tells the children that their life on earth has ended and their new life with him has begun.

"The term is over: the holidays have begun. The dream is ended: this is the morning."

And as He spoke He no longer looked to them like a lion; but the things that began to happen after that were so great and beautiful that I cannot write them. And for us this is the end of all the stories, and we can most truly say that they all lived happily ever after. But for them it was only the beginning of the real story. All their life in this world and all their adventures in Narnia had only been the cover and the title page: now at last they were beginning Chapter One of the Great Story, which no one on earth has read: which goes on forever: in which every chapter is better than the one before. [5]

I once experienced something like that through a song. The song was "Holy and Anointed One," and I was singing with a crowd of two to three thousand people at a conference my wife and I were attending. As we sang, the worship team sensed the presence of the Holy Spirit in the room and kept playing. The longer they played, the louder we sang. Tears streamed down my face as I sang more and more passionately. It was a euphoric sensation, one I had never had before or since. I never wanted the song to end.

Through that song came a moment of grace that is described in a scene from the movie *The Shawshank Redemption*. It is the scene in which one of the prison inmates, Tim Robbins, plays a recording of Mozart's *The Marriage of Figaro*, over the loudspeaker system. As the Italian duet sings, all the prisoners stop what they are doing to listen. In a voice-over, Morgan Freeman says: "I have no idea to this day what them two Italian ladies were singin' about. Truth is, I don't *want* to know. Some things are best left unsaid. I like to think they were singin' about something so beautiful it *can't* be expressed in words, and makes your heart ache because of it."

That's exactly how I felt as I was singing the song. It was something so beautiful it couldn't be expressed in words and made my heart ache because of it. What had been extended to me in that moment of grace was a taste of heaven.

That moment stirred within me a dare-to-dream longing that nothing on earth could satisfy. I felt like a child again, a carefree and happy child. I know it sounds like a fairy tale, but somewhere over the rainbow is a place where God lives, and sometime ago Jesus went there to prepare a place for us so that we could live there too.

Heaven is our home. That is what we have been homesick for all of our lives. And if we must become children in order to get there, as Jesus insisted, then maybe the best preparation for that is not to be found in colleges and seminaries but in places like Narnia and Oz. Maybe the longings to go there don't come from textbooks but from songs. And maybe if the longings are strong enough, anything might take us there for a glimpse—a wardrobe, a tornado, even a moment at the movies.

Conclusion

God is so passionate about molding us into the image of His Son that He will use any tool to accomplish that work. He will use a pastor one day, a filmmaker the next. One day he will use a professional counselor, the day after that a longtime friend. He may use a crisis, such as a death, or a celebration, such as a birth. He may use a sad country song, or a joyful song of praise. He may use a dream, or a daydream. He may even use our sin, the way He did in David's life. Or a moment of betrayal, the way He did in Peter's.

God is patient in making a masterpiece out of our lives, taking a lifetime if necessary. He is also persistent. He will stop at nothing, except our own unwillingness to cooperate. That is a boundary He has chosen not to cross. But it is the only boundary. Tragic circumstances won't stop Him. Physical limitations won't stop Him. Even satanic opposition won't stop Him.

It doesn't matter if life has shattered us, or some enemy, or even if we have caused the shattering ourselves. God reaches down, picks up the pieces, and uses them to make something beautiful.

That is who He is. That is what He does.

When we help with this wonderful work that God is doing in other people's lives, we become His fellow workers (1 Corinthians 3:9). At least a portion of our eternal rewards will be based on the quality of our work (vv. 10-14). So often when we think of rewards, we think of the Emmy Awards that recognize the quality in work that has been done for television. Or the Tonys, which recognize the same in the theater. Or the Grammys in music. Or the Academy Awards in motion pictures.

I watch two things on television every year. I watch the Final Four in college basketball. And the Academy Awards.

During some part of each year's Academy Awards ceremonies, time is set aside to remember those in the film industry who have died during the past year. This year's tribute (March 26, 2000) was introduced by the talented young actor Edward Norton.

The tribute began somberly with the words, IN MEMORIAM. The lights dimmed as photographs of the deceased were projected onto a large onstage screen. Some of deceased had only one photograph. Others had two, some even three. Subtitled over the bottom of the photographs were their names and the type of work they did. Here is the list of the deceased in the order they were shown.

Sylvia Sydney—actor
Jim Varney—actor
Ernest Gold—composer
Ruth Roman—actor
Henry Jones—actor
Robert Bresson—director
Desmond Lllewelyn—actor
Allan Carr—producer

Mario Puzo—screenwriter

Rory Calhoun—actor

Frank Tarloff—screenwriter

Mark Davis—animator

Hedy Lamarr—actor

Victor Mature—actor

Garson Kanin—screenwriter

Roger Vadim—producer/director

Mabel King—actor

Oliver Reed—actor

Albert Whitlock—special effects

Ian Bannen—actor

Abraham Polonsky—screenwriter

Dirk Bogarde—actor

Lila Kedrova—actor

Edward Dmytryk—director

Charles "Buddy" Rogers—actor

Madeline Kahn—actor

George C. Scott—actor

There was no applause for some of them, and only a sprinkling of it for several of the others. You could almost see people in the audience nudging one another, whispering things like, "Who was *she?*" "What did *he* write?" "Never heard of her." "Worked in silent films, I think."

Of course, there were ones they did remember. Ones even I remembered. Mario Puzo, for one, author of *The Godfather.* Hedy Lamarr, I had heard of her, too, though I couldn't tell you what films she starred in, but I knew she had starred in a lot. Madeline Kahn, we all remember her. She had three photographs. The one of her in *Young Frankenstein* got the most applause. Finally, George C. Scott. Who could forget him? He had three photos too. The first one was of him in a movie I hadn't seen. The second one was of him in *Dr. Strangelove*. The third one—cue theme music—was climactic. It was the one of him in his Academy Award–winning role as Patton, standing in front of a massive American flag that dwarfed him, poised to make that now-famous speech of his to the troops.

The applause suddenly swelled with the music, then just as suddenly receded with it.

Quick fade.

Cut to commercial.

The entire tribute lasted a little over three minutes. A lifetime of work, and each of them got six, maybe seven seconds of remembrance. Who of us even knew their names? Of the few who did, who of them could list their credits? And of the one or two that could, who of them knew anything about the person behind those credits, the *real* person? The audience didn't seem to know, and if they did, from the sound of the applause, didn't seem to care.

It was a poignant moment, at least for me. And I couldn't help wondering what the people in the audience were thinking. I wondered if they wondered how they would be remembered the year they passed away and a tribute like this was paid to them. Someday they will end up on a screen that begins with the words: IN MEMORIAM. Then it will be a whole new generation's turn to wonder about those people on the screen, who they were, what they did, and why it matters.

Judging from the applause, the gold on the Oscars is spread pretty thin. From God's perspective, even thinner still.

As far as eternity is concerned, it matters little whether we win a championship or lose it, whether we win the Pulitzer Prize or we don't, whether we win an Academy Award or we are snubbed by the Academy. And that is humbling to realize. But better to be humbled on earth than in heaven.

The work that is recognized by God and rewarded by Him is the work He is doing in us and through us in the lives of others. It is the serious work of God to mold us into the image of His Son. And He employs all sorts of workers to assist Him.

Even so menial a worker as a moment in the movies.

To put things in perspective, C.S. Lewis once said that all the books ever written would not be worth the salvation of a single soul.

The same could be said of all the movies ever produced.

I think all twenty-seven people on that list would agree.

I think they would now say that all the memorable movie moments they left behind wouldn't be worth the one moment of faith they took with them—or didn't.

And I think they would join the thief on the cross in saying that it isn't important *why* you are remembered, but by *whom*.

ENDNOTES

INTRODUCTION

1. C.S. Lewis, *The Screwtape Letters,* New York: Macmillan, 1976, p. 17.

2. Walker Percy, *The Moviegoer,* New York: Random House, 1960, p. 7.

THE MOVIES

HISTORY OF THE MOVIES

1. C.S. Lewis, *An Experiment in Criticism,* London: Cambridge University Press, 1961, pp. 137-138.

2. Aleksandr Solzhenitsyn, *East and West,* New York: Harper & Row, 1980, p. 5.

3. George Amberg, *The New York Times Film Reviews,* New York: New York Times Company, 1928, p. 72.

4. Susan Vaughn, "The Movie Palaces: Where Fantasies Replaced Real Life," *The Los Angeles Times,* California: 1992, p. E4.

TRUTH FROM THE MOVIES

1. Robert McKee, *Story,* New York: HarperCollins Publishers, 1997, p. 25.

CRITICISM OF THE MOVIES

1. Rainer Maria Rilke, *Letters to a Young Poet,* New York: W.W. Norton & Company, 1934, p. 32.

2. J.B. Phillips, *The New Testament in Modern English,* London: Geoffrey Bles, 1960, pp. viii-ix.

3. C.S. Lewis, *An Experiment in Criticism,* London: Cambridge University Press, 1961, p. 19.

MOMENTS AT THE MOVIES

1. John Brady, *The Craft of the Screenwriter,* New York: Simon & Schuster, 1981, p. 377.

2. Duane Byrge, compiler, *Private Screenings,* Atlanta: Turner Publishing, 1995, pp. 7-8.

3. Ibid., p. 48.

4. Ibid., p. 12.

5. Aleksandr Solzhenitsyn, *East and West,* New York: Harper & Row, 1980, p. 6.

6. C.S. Lewis, *The Problem of Pain,* New York: Macmillan, 1962, pp. 42-43.

7. Noah benShea, *Jacob's Journey,* New York: Random House, 1991, pp. 43-44.

REFLECTIONS ON SPECIFIC MOVIES

REFLECTIONS ON *BAMBI*

1. William Goldman, *Adventures in the Screen Trade,* New York: Warner Books, 1983, p. 154.

2. Roger Ebert, *Roger Ebert's Movie Home Companion 1990 Edition,* Kansas City: Andrews and McMeel, 1989, p. 53.

3. David Rosenberg, editor, *The Movie That Changed My Life,* New York: Penguin Books, 1991, p. 4.

4. C.S. Lewis, *An Experiment in Criticism,* London: Cambridge University Press, 1961, p. 137.

5. Felix Salten, *Bambi,* New York: Grosset & Dunlap, 1929, p. 34.

6. Ibid., p. 35.

7. Ibid., pp. 124-125.

8. Ibid., p. 126.

REFLECTIONS ON *CAMELOT*

1. Robert McKee, *Story,* New York: HarperCollins Publishers, 1997, p. 12.

2. Henry Gilbert, *King Arthur,* New York: The Saalfield Publishing Co., n.d., p. 9.

REFLECTIONS ON *AMADEUS*

1. Elie Wiesel, *Night,* New York: Bantam, 1982, p. 2.

2. Don Campbell, *The Mozart Effect,* New York: Avon Books, 1997, p. 28.

REFLECTIONS ON *FIELD OF DREAMS*

1. Karl Schanzer and Thomas Lee Wright, *American Screenwriters,* New York: Avon Books, 1993, p. 185.

REFLECTIONS ON *ORDINARY PEOPLE*

1. Gary Solomon, *The Motion Picture Prescription,* Santa Rosa, California: Aslan Publishing, 1995, p. 146.

2. Anne Lamott, *Bird by Bird,* New York: Anchor Books, 1994, p. 32.

REFLECTIONS ON *SAVING PRIVATE RYAN*

1. Peter Bogdanovich, *The Best American Movie Writing 1999,* New York: St. Martin's Griffin, 1999, p. 109.

2. Jesse Kornbluth and Linda Sunshine, editors, *Now You Know,* New York: Newmarket Press, 1999, p. 96.

3. Ibid., p. 75.

4. Ibid., p. 61.

5. Ibid., p. 112.

6. Ibid., p. 45.

REFLECTIONS ON *SMOKE*

1. Wayne Wang, *Smoke and Blue in the Face,* New York: Hyperion, 1990, p. 13.

2. Frederick Buechner, *The Sacred Journey,* New York: Harper & Row, 1982, p. 7.

REFLECTIONS ON *HOOSIERS*

1. Roger Ebert, *Roger Ebert's Movie Home Companion 1990 Edition,* Kansas City: Andrews and McMeel, 1989, p. 348.

REFLECTIONS ON *HOOP DREAMS*

1. Roger Ebert, *Roger Ebert's Movie Home Companion 1990 Edition,* Kansas City: Andrews and McMeel, 1989, p. 324.

2. Interview with Peter Gilbert, *Mars Hill Review,* Littleton, Colorado: Number 2/May 1995, p. 154.

3. Steve James quoted on the Internet site: <http://www.tlt.com/hoop/hdsynops.htm>, 1995 by Fine Line Features.

REFLECTIONS ON *THE ELEPHANT MAN*

1. Pauline Kael, *Taking It All In,* New York: Holt, Rinehart and Winston, 1984, p. 82.

2. George F. Will, *The Morning After,* New York: Macmillan, Inc., 1986, p. 101.

3. Pauline Kael, *Hooked,* New York: E.P. Dutton, 1989, p. 88.

4. Ibid., p. 176.

5. Ibid., p. 169.

6. Kael, *Taking It All In*, pp. 246-47.

7. Ibid., pp. 83, 85.

REFLECTIONS ON *THE DEAD POETS SOCIETY*

1. Linda Seger and Edward Jay Whetmore, *From Script to Screen,* New York: Henry Holt and Company, 1994, pp. 9, 95.

2. Ibid., p. 95.

3. Dietrich Bonhoeffer, quoted in the preface to *The Cost of Discipleship*, New York: The Macmillan Company, 1959.

REFLECTIONS ON *AMISTAD*

1. Flannery O'Connor, *Mystery and Manners,* New York: Farrar, Straus & Giroux, 1969, p. 118.

REFLECTIONS ON *SHINDLER'S LIST*

1. Michael Berenbaum, *The World Must Know,* Boston: Little, Brown and Company, 1993, dedication page.

2. Ibid., p. 219.

3. Aleksandr Solzhenitsyn, *East and West*, New York: Harper & Row, 1980, p. 19.

REFLECTIONS ON *THE WIZARD OF OZ*

1. Frederick Buechner, *The Sacred Journey,* New York: Harper & Row, 1982, pp. 14-15.

2. Edward Hoffman, *Visions of Innocence,* Boston: Shambhala Publications, Inc., 1992, pp. 103-104.

3. Salman Rushdie, *The Wizard of Oz*, London: British Film Institute, 1995, p. 23.

4. C.S. Lewis, *The Problem of Pain,* New York: The Macmillan Company, 1970, p. 144.

5. C.S. Lewis, *The Last Battle*, New York: The Macmillan Company, 1956, pp. 173-174.

RECOMMENDED READING

Among the books listed below, I have included a few compilations by two film critics whose reviews I read and opinions I respect.

The one is the popular critic Roger Ebert. I say "popular" because he writes reviews for the *Chicago Sun-Times* that are syndicated in newspapers across the country, and he hosts the television show *Roger Ebert & the Movies,* which is also nationally syndicated. His reviews are compiled in a collection that is revised annually.

The other reviewer is Pauline Kael, who spent her career writing film reviews for the *New Yorker,* a literary magazine whose readership is smaller and more esoteric.

I enjoy Roger Ebert because he will often champion a small independent film like *Hoop Dreams.* Regardless of the reviews, the summer blockbusters will always attract an audience, but films like *Hoop Dreams* won't unless they get some degree of national exposure. That is how a critic can help, and no critic, in my opinion, has been more helpful to that cause than Roger Ebert.

Roger Ebert will overlook a lot in a film if he likes it, and I appreciate that about him. Pauline Kael overlooks nothing. In my opinion, that is both her strength as a critic and her weakness. Even so, I am indebted to her for sharpening my eye when it comes to seeing movies.

If you want to get just a few good books to help you become more skilled in observing movies, let me suggest the following in the order I would purchase them. I would start off with C.S. Lewis' *An Experiment in*

Criticism. It is one of his more obscure books but is filled with insight in how to approach any work of art.

The second book I would want in my library would be K.L. Billingsley's *The Seductive Image,* subtitled: "A Christian Critique of the World of Film." It is a good, balanced introduction to film from a Christian perspective.

Next I would get the most recent copy of Roger Ebert's *Video Companion* and Pauline Kael's *For Keeps,* which is a sampling of reviews over her thirty-year career.

Then I would start working my way through all of Linda Seger's books. She is a script consultant, and her books are full of insightful interviews with screenwriters and directors. I think I would start with *Making a Good Script Great.* It will help you to think like a screenwriter and make you a more perceptive viewer, drawing your attention to things like theme, motifs, character development, plot, and subplots.

Books

American Film Institute with Duane Byrge, *Private Screenings.* Atlanta, Georgia: Turner Publishing, Inc., 1995.

Billingsley, K.L., *The Seductive Image.* Westchester, Illinois: Crossway Books, 1989.

Ebert, Roger, *Roger Ebert's Video Companion 1999 Edition* (published yearly). Kansas City, Missouri: Andrews and McMeel, 1998.

Jewett, Robert, *Saint Paul at the Movies.* Louisville, Kentucky: Westminster/John Knox Press, 1993.

Kael, Pauline, *Deeper into Movies.* Boston, Massachusetts: Little, Brown, 1973.

Kael, Pauline, *For Keeps.* New York, New York: E.P. Dutton, 1996.

Kael, Pauline, *Hooked.* New York, New York: E. P. Dutton, 1989.

Kael, Pauline, *Movie Love.* New York, New York: Penguin Books, 1991.

Kael, Pauline, *State of the Art.* New York, New York: E.P. Dutton, 1985.

Kael, Pauline, *Taking It All In.* New York, New York: Holt, Rinehart and Winston, 1984.

Lewis, C.S., *An Experiment in Criticism.* London, England: Cambridge University Press, 1973.

Malone, Peter, *Movie Christs and Antichrists.* New York, New York: Crossroad Publishing Company, 1990.

Martin, Joel W. and Conrad E. Ostwalt Jr., editors, *Screening the Sacred.* Boulder, Colorado: Westview Press, 1995.

O'Brien, Tom, *The Screening of America.* New York, New York: Continuum, 1990.

Rosenberg, David, editor, *The Movie That Changed My Life.* New York, New York: Penguin Books, 1991.

Schanzer, Karl, and Thomas Lee Wright, *American Screenwriters.* New York, New York: Avon Books, 1993.

Scott, Bernard Brandon, *Hollywood Dreams and Biblical Stories.* Minneapolis, Minnesota: Augsburg Fortress Publishers, 1994.

Seger, Linda, *The Art of Adaptation: Turning Fact and Fiction into Film.* New York, New York: Henry Holt and Company, 1992.

Seger, Linda, *Creating Unforgettable Characters.* New York, New York: Henry Holt and Company, 1990.

Seger, Linda and Edward Jay Whetmore, *From Script to Screen.* New York, New York: Henry Holt and Company, 1994.

Seger, Linda, *Making a Good Script Great.* New York, New York: Dodd, Mead and Company, 1987.

Sinetar, Marsha, *Reel Power.* Liguori, Missouri: Triumph Books, 1993.

Solomon, Gary, *The Motion Picture Prescription.* Santa Rosa, California: Aslan Publishing, 1995.

Periodicals

Creative Screenwriting is a quarterly publication of the finest selection of screenwriting articles and reviews. Subscriptions can be ordered at (800) 788-1323, fax (213) 851-8644, or by writing Script Source, Inc., P.O. Box 46393, West Hollywood, CA 90046.

Mars Hill Review is an excellent quarterly periodical of essays, studies, and reminders of God. Subscriptions can be ordered by calling (800) 990-MARS or by writing to *Mars Hill Review*, 11757 W. Ken Caryl F330, Littleton, CO 80127-3700.

Script is published bimonthly especially for screenwriters by Forum, Inc., 5683 Sweet Air Rd., Baldwin, MD 21013-9009, telephone: (410) 592-3466, fax: (410) 592-8062.

MOVIE CREDITS

Bambi
From the book, *Bambi,* by Felix
Salten
Supervising direction: David D.
Hand
Story direction: Perce Pearce
Story adaption: Larry Morey

Camelot
Based on the book, *The Once and
Future King,* by T.H. White
And the play, *Camelot,* play and
lyrics by Alan Jay Lerner, music by
Frederick Loewe
Produced by Jack L Warner
Directed by Joshua Logan
Screenplay and lyrics by Alan Jay
Lerner
Music by Frederick Loewe
Starring Richard Harris (Arthur),
Vanessa Redgrave (Guenevere),
Franco Nero (Lancelot)

Amadeus
Produced by Saul Zaentz
Directed by Milos Forman
Screenplay by Peter Shaffer
Starring F. Murray Abraham
(Salieri), Tom Hulce (Mozart)

Field of Dreams
Produced by Lawrence Gordon and
Charles Gordon
Directed by Phil Alden Robinson
Screenplay by Phil Alden Robinson
Starring Kevin Coster (Ray
Kinsella), Amy Madigan (Annie

Kinsella), Gaby Hoffman (Karin
Kinsella) Ray Liotta (Shoeless Joe
Jackson), Timothy Busfield (Mark),
James Earl Jones (Terence Mann),
Burt Lancaster (Dr. "Moonlight"
Graham), Dwier Brown (John
Kinsella)

Ordinary People
Produced by Ronald L. Schwary
Directed by Robert Redford
Screenplay by Alvin Sargent
Starring Donald Sutherland
(Calvin), Mary Tyler Moore (Beth),
Judd Hirsch (Berger), Timothy
Hutton (Conrad)

Saving Private Ryan
Produced by Steven Spielberg, Ian
Bryce, Mark Gordon, and Gary
Levinsohn
Directed by Steven Speilberg
Screenplay by Robert Rodat
Starring Tom Hanks (Captain John
Miller), Matt Damon (Private James
Ryan)

Smoke
Produced by Greg Johnson, Peter
Newman, Kenzo Harikoshi, and
Hisami Kuroiwa
Directed by Wayne Wang
Screenplay by Paul Auster
Starring William Hurt (Paul
Benjamin), Harvey Keitel (Auggie
Wren)

Hoosiers
Produced by Carter De Haven and Angelo Pizzo
Directed by David Anspaugh
Screenplay by Angelo Pizzo
Starring Gene Hackman (Norman Dale), Barbara Hershey (Myra Fleener), Dennis Hopper (Shooter)

Hoop Dreams
Produced by Frederick Marx, Steve James, and Peter Gilbert
Directed by Steve James
Screenplay by Steve James, Frederick Marx, and Peter Gilbert

The Elephant Man
Executive producer: Stuart Cornfeld
Produced by Jonathan Sanger
Directed by David Lynch
Screenplay by Christopher DeVore, Eric Bergen, and David Lynch
Starring Anthony Hopkins (Dr. Frederick Treves), John Hurt (John Merrick), Anne Bancroft (Mrs. Kendal), John Gielgud (Mr. Carr-Gomm)

The Dead Poets Society
Produced by Steven Haft, Paul Junger Witt, and Tony Thomas
Directed by Peter Weir
Screenplay by Tom Schulman
Starring Robin Williams (John Keating), Robert Sean Leonard (Neil Perry), Ethan Hawke (Todd Anderson)

Amistad
Produced by Steven Spielberg, Debbie Allen, and Colin Wilson
Directed by Steven Spielberg
Screenplay by David Franzoni
Starring Morgan Freeman, Anthony Hopkins, Djimon Hounsou, and Matthew McConaughey

Schindler's List
Based on the novel, *Schindler's List*, by Thomas Keneally
Executive producer: Kathleen Kennedy
Produced by Steven Spielberg, Gerald R. Moln, and Branko Lustig
Directed by Steven Spielberg
Screenplay by Steven Zallian
Starring Liam Neeson (Oskar Schindler), Ben Kingsley (Itzhak Stern), Ralph Fiennes (Amon Goeth)

The Wizard of Oz
Based on the book, *The Wizard of Oz*, by L. Frank Baum
Produced by Mervyn LeRoy
Directed by Victor Fleming
Screenplay by Noel Langley, Florence Ryerson, and Edgar Allan Woolf
Starring Judy Garland (Dorothy), Frank Morgan (The Wizard), Ray Bolger (Scarecrow), Bert Lahr (Cowardly Lion), Jack Haley (Tin Man), Billie Burke (Glinda, the Good Witch), Margaret Hamilton (The Wicked Witch)